Praise for *White Supremacy through Black Eyes*

This is one of the most eloquent, thoughtful books on racism and its legacies that I have ever read. Beverly Eileen Mitchell explores white supremacy in all its forms as a sin, a theological defacement of how God intends human beings to live with one another. Our violation of God's intent has caused immeasurable anguish for one another and for our country. Mitchell has written a quietly impassioned plea to see each other as we truly are—human beings all created in God's image—so that we can finally flourish individually and as a country.

—**Victoria J. Barnett**, general editor, Dietrich Bonhoeffer Works, English Edition

White Supremacy through Black Eyes makes the construct of a racist ideology more visible, less elusive. Mitchell interrogates the interpersonal and corporate dynamics that sustain the practices of global inequality. Through theological reflection and critique, the reader will encounter in this book a thoughtful and compelling invitation to see the world for what it is and to change it for the good.

—**Adam L. Bond**, author of *The Imposing Preacher: Samuel DeWitt Proctor and Black Public Faith* and associate professor of religion and African American studies, Baylor University

White Supremacy through Black Eyes deepens Mitchell's rich and substantive theological interrogation of the systematic evils of division, discord, and oppression in human experiences, found throughout her work. In this text, Mitchell calls anyone with a passion for racial healing and justice to embrace a theological framing of metanoia as the path toward reconciliation and a justice rooted in the hope of the Christian witness. If we are going to heal the brokenness of our world around race and issues of human dignity, we will need to attend to the theological roots of those divisions.

—**Asa J. Lee**, president and professor for theological formation for ministry, Pittsburgh Theological Seminary

In *White Supremacy through Black Eyes*, theologian Beverly Eileen Mitchell makes the claim that white supremacy is, at its root, a theological problem. If we are made in the image and likeness of God, the sin of defacement—the assault on the dignity of another—is a form of idolatry that breaks the commandment to love both God and neighbor. In this thoughtful book, Mitchell integrates a lifetime of experience, research, and reflection to offer a frank discussion of the damage that the ideology of white supremacy inflicts upon Black people and others on the lower rungs of the social ladder. Mitchell gently but firmly guides readers along to understand the spiritual commitment needed to reckon with history and move toward repairing the injustice of racism before any hope of racial reconciliation can emerge. This book will serve theological students, scholars, and congregations alike. Professor Mitchell opens her mind to us, offering a clear and compelling vision of the constructive engagement needed to move forward along the path of racial healing.

—**Mary Clark Moschella**, Roger J. Squire Professor of Pastoral Care and Counseling at Yale Divinity School and author of *Narrative Spiritual Care: Theory and Practice* (UNC Press, forthcoming)

Beverly Eileen Mitchell admits, and rightfully so, this is not the kind of book that a theologian wants to write but it is one that must be written and read. This book speaks truthfully about the ideology and idolatry of racism that has torn the fabric of human-to-human and divine-human relationships. Mitchell's work is not only a critique of racism and its detrimental effects but also a construction of ethics, a practical eight-step guide, for communities of faith desiring to play a major role in the work of racial reconciliation and social justice.

—**Frederick L. Ware**, professor of theology and associate dean Howard University School of Divinity, Washington, DC, and author of *African American Theology: An Introduction*

White Supremacy through Black Eyes

White Supremacy through Black Eyes

Human Dignity, Defacement, and the Grace of Racial Healing

Beverly Eileen Mitchell

FORTRESS PRESS
MINNEAPOLIS

WHITE SUPREMACY THROUGH BLACK EYES
Human Dignity, Defacement, and the Grace of Racial Healing

30 29 28 27 26 25 1 2 3 4 5 6 7 8 9

Library of Congress Control Number: 2025936102 (print)

Cover image: African-American nurse and child, between 1900 and 1915, Missouri History Museum; African American woman, half-length portrait, facing slightly right, 1900, photographic print from Daniel Murray Collection (Library of Congress); Photograph of John W. Jones, before 1900; Portrait of an unidentified African American laborer, 1946, Photographer/Studio: Louise Putman, Courtesy of Missouri State Archives; Face of an young black woman in black and white, from AND-ONE/Getty Images; Boy in Polo Shirt Greyscale Portrait, Photo by Pixabay: https://www.pexels.com/photo/boy-in-polo-shirt-greyscale-portrait-141651/
Cover design: Kris E. Miller

Print ISBN: 979-8-8898-3442-7
eBook ISBN: 979-8-8898-3443-4

In loving memory of
Marvin Mitchell (1931–2017)
and Edwina S. Mitchell (1932–2013),
my beloved parents

Contents

Acknowledgments

I am grateful to Wesley Theological Seminary for the sabbatical that gave me the time to devote to this project in the 2020–2021 academic year. I want to thank Dr. Carla Works, academic dean, for her interest and genuine encouragement. I am also grateful to my faculty of Wesley Theological Seminary for their continued support and interest in my work.

I am deeply indebted to Hope Cooper for her assistance in obtaining interlibrary loans for pertinent books and articles. No matter how many requests I made in a day, she sent me my requests in the same day! Her professionalism, expertise, and ready support were of invaluable help.

I am very grateful for the unfailing support of the Fortress Press team who worked with me on this project, Dr. Laura Gifford, Louise Spencely, Lisa Eaton, and Kris E. Miller, for their roles in getting this manuscript to press. Special thanks goes to Dr. Gifford, for her guidance, insightful suggestions, and steadfast support, which helped me to see this work to its completion.

I also wish to thank Dr. Quentin Graham and Dr. F. Victor Rovira for their invaluable assistance as thoughtful, quality conversation partners, whose interest in this project spurred me on until the task was done.

I have had a host of supporters who encouraged me frequently, commiserated with me, prayed for me; and rejoiced with me when I reached my goal. I will not name names but they and I know who they are.

Finally, I am most appreciative of my two sisters, Joyce and Janice, for being my biggest cheerleaders, unflinching truth-tellers, as well as my dearest friends.

Preface

I was born the same year that Rosa Parks defied a segregation law prohibiting Blacks from remaining seated on public transportation when a white person was entitled to the seat. This was not the first time she had defied the segregation law regarding public transportation, but December 3, 1955, was the moment in time when a constellation of things was in place, such that her defiance that evening would be a major catalyst that would spark a mass freedom movement. That fortuitous movement would not only catapult the young Black minister, the Rev. Dr. Martin Luther King Jr., into leadership of a movement that galvanized seemingly insignificant members of the Black masses. For a relatively short period of time, the Civil Rights Movement raised the hopes of Black people who were "sick and tired of being sick and tired," inspiring them with the notion that maybe *this* time their deliverance from a relentless, dehumanizing, humiliating subservience to whites would finally come to an end.[1]

1 The "sick and tired" phrase has been attributed to civil rights activist Fannie Lou Hamer.

By the time I was eight years old, the Civil Rights Movement (1955–1968) was well underway. In May of 1963, Black high school students and youth gathered at Kelly Ingram Park in Birmingham to launch a protest against the humiliating practice of segregation legally enshrined in the Plessy v. Ferguson US Supreme Court decision of 1896. The infamous public safety commissioner at the time, Eugene "Bull" Connor, was intent on breaking up the gathered crowd of "lawless demonstrators" by ordering Birmingham police and firemen to disperse the crowd. The police sicced their police dogs onto the crowd, leaving the youth to duck and dodge the menacing dogs, who tore their clothes and threatened to bite them. Firemen turned their water hoses on the youth, who were then swept down the street by the force of gallons of water tearing at their clothes, so powerful that youth were swept along the sidewalk. No doubt frightened, they clutched futilely at the huge store windows and doors of commercial shops in hopes of getting away from the cascading water that rendered them like human ragdolls. After all these years, my eight-year-old self remembers the bewildering sight, wondering what on earth Black people could have done to unleash the venom and hatred worn on the faces of the white police officers and firemen. But somehow, after several decades, I had buried the sound of the screams of the youth and children.

It took sixty years, but through the constant replay of the fatal encounter of George Floyd, I finally remembered the sound of the screams of the Birmingham youth. Watching the replay of the handling of Floyd by law enforcement in June 2020 too many times before I shut it off, I also remembered the bewilderment, anxiety, and the queasy feeling in the pit of my stomach that I had felt in 1963. I finally understood why George Floyd's death was particularly traumatic: It had triggered previous trauma from childhood.

Once I understood the connection between what I remembered and what I was reliving, I felt the rage. Even with the passage of time since George Floyd's death, the rage has not fully dissipated. So, to find meaning in this present experience of racial conflict, I have written about the clash between basic human dignity and commonplace white supremacy. This is not exactly the book I had initially planned to write; but it is the book that needed to be written.

Introduction

Since this country's inception, white supremacy has been the ruling ideology that governs the treatment of diverse peoples who are classified as "non-white." Consequently, the African American struggle for justice has been a long-standing struggle for the acknowledgment of and respect for their dignity as fully human beings, made in the image of God. Two significant historical moments, one in the nineteenth century and the other in the twentieth century, raised the hopes of Black people in America after emancipation in 1865. During the Reconstruction era, Congress ratified three constitutional amendments which granted the rights of full citizenship to African Americans after nearly three centuries of enslavement. However, white resistance to Black progress robbed the latter of the fulfillment of their status as full-fledged participants in the American experiment and as contributing members of society. Instead, because of white supremacy, Black people were *re*-shackled by nearly one hundred years of legalized segregation, which constricted not only their freedom to flourish, but which was the denial of dignity that would hamstring a people from fulfilling their full potential as human beings.

Because of the color of their skin, they experienced nearly one hundred years of wearing the shackles of segregation and its attendant violence, threats of more violence, and deprivation of opportunities, accompanied by a pariah status in a country whose citizens constantly thwarted their efforts to excel. However, Black people did not live their lives sitting by and hoping for a change to come. Throughout the one hundred years of their emancipation, they struggled against white supremacy by resisting internalizing the dominant message of their "innate inferiority." Amid the pressure of that resistance, and despite the threats of violence, a major movement erupted because African Americans were sick and tired of being sick and tired. They did so with the help of charismatic leadership and foot soldiers who were willing to risk their lives to be (truly) free.

The Civil Rights Movement burst forth on the scene, taking the position of eschewing retaliatory violence, but was nevertheless resolute in its commitment to social change. Once again, hopes were raised that the aspirations of Black people, with their sociopolitical and economic gains, could lead to a fulfillment of what Reconstruction had promised to do. However, both Reconstruction and the Civil Rights Movement were doomed to fall short. Neither movement addressed the underlying *ideology* that would foil the promise of full freedom. Despite important changes brought about by Reconstruction and the Civil Rights Movement, neither of them conquered the underlying ideology of death: white supremacy.

I contend that the underlying root of white supremacy is theological. Without the recognition that the nature of white supremacy is theological, our efforts to dismantle it will be limited by measures such as sociopolitical, economic, and psychological approaches, or a combination/integration of these disciplines, as these can only go so far. What makes an approach theological is an understanding of who and what human beings are in terms of their interrelations with each other, and their relations of the One who has created them. Theology, as a discipline that addresses the "spirit of the human," that is, what makes people human, what motivates humans to do what they do, and who we are, is essential. We ourselves must discover the extent to which we *can* challenge white supremacy, which is an ideology that runs deep and expands widely in terms of how it hinders our ability to be centered on the welfare of all, as opposed to a focus on only ourselves.

Our goal is transformation in terms of the way we perceive and engage each other as fellow human beings. It takes transformation to be able to walk into the truth that we all have been created in the image of God, which makes us holy siblings. By faith, living into that theological reality, our concerns will be centered on the welfare of all of us, not simply our own.

Chapter 1 establishes a Jewish–Christian theological grounding for human dignity. My concept of human dignity is drawn from the first chapter of Genesis, in which the biblical text informs us that the human being is created in the image of God. The elaboration of what constitutes human dignity will be established through my engagement with the work of Raimond Gaita and Simone Weil. I contend that human dignity is granted to all, and has both socio-ethical and political dimensions to it because of our interrelatedness to all other human beings through our mutual bearing of God's image. Through recognizing our sacred worth, we are called to live out of our ethical responsibility to all. The image of God, given to all of us, ties us to each other. By living out of our ethical responsibility to all, we see the ideology of white supremacy as a troubling example of insufficiently challenged beliefs, attitudes, and conduct that are reflective of white superiority, and we unmask the toxic, theological pretensions of racial supremacy. In this discussion of how racial superiority is long-standing and manifested in ordinary human interactions across racial lines, I discuss the degree to which white supremacy takes on a religious cast that makes it extremely difficult to dismantle racist practices.

In chapter 2, I define the word "defacement" as the violation of human dignity. The work of Emmanuel Levinas, Raimond Gaita, and Simone Weil informs my discussion of defacement. This chapter establishes that the sin of defacement is in individuals, but even more clearly is manifested as a communal phenomenon. I highlight the harm of defacement, and the 2020 killing of George Floyd by police officers as a concrete example of defacement.

In chapter 3, I explore what happens after I establish the theological basis for what makes us human and ties us to each other. In this discussion of how racial superiority is long-standing and manifested in ordinary human interactions across racial lines, I discuss the degree to which white supremacy's religious cast makes it extremely difficult to dismantle racist practices simply through sociopolitical means. Because white supremacy is at its core a spiritual problem, our activism against it must have a religious/spiritual component to cut this ideology at its roots. The work of George Kelsey informs this discussion through his assertion that racism constitutes a "rival" faith, and, therefore, it is idolatrous; it also corrupts our relationships with God, other humans, and ourselves.

In chapter 4, I examine some of the impediments to fruitful engagement in the work of repairing the racial breach caused by white supremacy. This chapter highlights some of the difficulties of why it is challenging to address white supremacy in the public square. I argue that the responsibility of doing the "heavy" lifting of challenging white supremacy has been laid upon minorities, and that it is essential that, for the sake of non-whites and the dominant racial group, whites must address white supremacy. It has been left to people who are minorities to address, with some whites joining them as "allies." Rather, it is the minoritized people of color that are the allies of *whites*. Reflecting on the work of James Baldwin, Richard Wright, W. E. B. DuBois, and Toni Morrison, I contend that the "problem" of race or white supremacy is one that white people must take on. Some whites seek to engage in healthy cross-racial relationships, because they believe it is the right thing to do. However, there are well-intentioned white "allies" who are eager to rush into a discussion on "reconciliation" while eschewing the inner work required to renounce white supremacy (and all that goes with it). Only through the rejection of the fantasy of white superiority and an avowal of communal reckoning with unaddressed injustices, which continue to feed inequality of access to opportunities and resources, can their allyship be perceived as engagement in the fight for justice in a serious, constructive way.

In chapter 5, I maintain that racial reconciliation is a process, and that individual and communal healing work are essential prerequisites for preparing ourselves and others for the commitment to authentic racial reconciliation. That healing work involves reckoning with our nation's past, and renouncing attitudes, beliefs, and practices that nurture and sustain white supremacy. Finally, I close with eight steps that I believe will help to liberate us from perpetuating white supremacy and the practices that feed it.

CHAPTER 1

Human Dignity and Sacred Worth

On that day, in the spring of 1963, I asked my mother, "Why do 'they' hate us so much?," because what I saw disturbed me. I knew that it was wrong, though I didn't understand why. I had already recognized that the world was divided between "us" and "them." I knew that I was an "us." I also came to know what provoked it. In the mind of an eight-year-old child, I truly wanted to know what "we" had done to prompt that kind of violent reaction from white policemen. I never have fathomed what we could have done. I still don't comprehend how fellow human beings could do that to another. Teenaged youth and children were out protesting in the streets because they were tired of having their dignity trampled on. But the "why" of the question remains. What was it about *us* that made people think that the constant assault on our dignity was "okay"? I have yet to find a satisfactory answer. I have come to the conclusion that the police officers giving their dogs the signal to attack the youth was morally wrong. I have also come to the conclusion that the firemen were also morally wrong to train their fire hoses on the young protesters. The Black people of Birmingham wanted the recognition of their human dignity acknowledged and respected.

THE ANCHOR FOR OUR HUMANNESS

I have chosen to anchor our discussion of what it means to be human in a theological framework which establishes a transcendent grounding for human existence. Because we humans are incapable of attaining perfection as creatures due to our propensity to sin against God and each other, a transcendent grounding is necessary to safeguard that which makes it possible for us to enjoy holy fellowship with God and with each other. The possibility for such fellowship with the Divine comes to us as a divine gift; that we might be in communion with God and fellow human beings is made possible for us despite our creaturely finitude and our propensity to sin.[1] As Reinhold Niebuhr once observed, it is the finitude,

1 Our finitude, with the limitations that arise from that, is not sin itself. Rather, the root of our propensity to sin lies in our refusal to *embrace* our creatureliness and overstep the bounds. This interpretation of our condition before God has been treated by Reinhold Niebuhr, in *The Nature and Destiny of Man, A Christian Interpretation*, vol. 1 (Scribner's Sons, 1964) and Matt Jenson, *The Gravity of Sin, Augustine, Luther and Barth on homo incurvatus in se* (T&T Clark, 2006).

dependence, and insufficiency of humanity's earthly life "are facts which belong to God's plan of creation," and should be accepted with reverence and deep humility.[2]

GOD'S TRANSCENDENCE AS THE SAFEGUARD OF HUMAN DIGNITY

It is the transcendence of the divine that safeguards the dignity of all human beings, regardless of race/ethnicity, national origin, sexual orientation, gender identification, class, level of education or the lack thereof, intellectual capacity, religious orientation, and so on. If the determination as to whether a person or group has value and worth is left up to fellow human beings, we are all rendered completely vulnerable to the caprice, whim, or the ill will of flawed humans. I acknowledge that my insistence on transcendence would suggest a less than optimistic view of human nature. However, my study of history and my own personal observations of human behavior support the conclusion that there are human beings, individually and collectively, who have no qualms whatsoever about denying or violating the dignity of other human beings.

A discussion of human dignity, which applies to all human beings, affirms that we all have been blessed by not only life itself, but also by bearing God's image in us, and this ratifies our sacred worth. Fortunately, sacred worth is a gift

2 Niebuhr, *The Nature and Destiny of Man*, 167.

that we do not earn. It is a gratuitous act of God in divine freedom. This generosity of God, such that God shares a part of God's very self with us freely, through our dignity as full human beings, establishes that none of us can rightly claim that we or our tribe of human beings is "superior" to other tribes, such that either we or they can claim superiority for ourselves, or our tribe, or our nation. There is no lawful basis upon which, in our delusion of superiority, we can justify ourselves with a bogus claim that we are superior and, based on this, claim the right to exercise coercion and dominance against others. Nor can we claim, in the name of God or in the name of anything else we worship as a god, the material resources of life and hoard access to opportunities for ourselves and our kin alone, and deny access to those resources and opportunities to others because we perceive them to be unworthy or view them as inferior to ourselves. In the most important aspect of our existence, the image of God in us and the dignity that arises from that image, we can recognize that though we humans are endowed with a variety of talents, gifts, and graces, they are given for us to *share* with others.

Those who take exception to a religious framework for human dignity are free to "translate" my concept of dignity into secular terms. There is a debate regarding whether human dignity is inherently "religious." Given my "requirements" for an equitable notion of human dignity, I suspect that the concept of human dignity may well be *inherently* religious. However, this does not preclude others from articulating a "secular" notion of human dignity from a framework of their own choosing. The only question would be whether there is a way to safeguard that dignity and whether it applies to all people, so that we are all protected from people or forces that do not recognize our inherent worth and connection to each other.

THE HUMAN BEING AS THE CULMINATION OF GOD'S CREATIVE EFFORT

Some contemporary theologians, such as Jürgen Moltmann, maintain that the Sabbath, not the human creature, is the culmination of God's creative effort. Moltmann's aim is to safeguard the deep tie between the human creature and the rest of creation because of his ecological concerns.[3]

Without denying the importance of theological attention to ecology, the life struggle of Black people of African descent in the United States has been the continual denial of their full humanity as humans created in the image of God, and the dignity that arises from bearing God's image, acknowledged, respected, and honored as one would claim for oneself. So, the elevation of the status of the Sabbath—which was made for human beings, not the reverse (Mark 2:27)—is a theological move that elevates "creation" at the expense of the human being. Because of the persistent denial of the

3 Jürgen Moltmann, *God in Creation: A New Theology of Creation and the Spirit of God*, 2nd ed. (Fortress Press, 1993), 276–297.

dignity and worth of Black people, I think that elevation of the Sabbath over the human creature fails to recognize the deep challenge there is for those whose full humanness is persistently denied or called into question. For people of African descent, it is important to keep in the forefront of our interactions with people that we expect to be treated in a way that acknowledges our full humanity.

Our creaturely existence has value and worth that is intended to be acknowledged, celebrated, and protected. The finitude that characterizes individual existence is a quality that describes the nature of our collective and national life as well. What precludes the fragmentary character of human life, whether individual or corporate, from being regarded as evil in biblical faith is that such life is to be understood from the perspective that each life and its meaning is connected to a divine plan that is in keeping with the will of God the Creator. Thus, even though in both the Hebrew Bible and the New Testament we are reminded often of the brevity and fragility of life, the created world and what dwells therein is deemed "good." Its intrinsic goodness arises solely from the reality that God is the "author" of the "good creation."[4]

There is more to what the biblical witness affirms about the nature of the human being before God (*coram deo*) that is of great significance to us as we reflect upon the value of human life in an age in which that value is not always recognized, affirmed, or protected. In the first account of

4 Daniel Migliore, *Faith Seeking Understanding: An Introduction to Christian Theology*, 2nd ed. (Wm. B. Eerdmans, 2004), 29.

creation in the book of Genesis, the biblical writer affirms in chapter 1 the following notion of the human creature before God: "Then God said, 'And let us make humankind in our image, according to our likeness'" (v. 26 NRSV). At the command of God, at the speaking of the Divine word, the human being was created in the "image" and the "likeness" of God. The Hebrew Bible and the New Testament maintain the importance of this initial affirmation about the human creature. Humanity did not create itself. God freely chose to create and the human being is the culmination of God's creative efforts. And God pronounced this "very good" (Gen 1:25, 31 NRSV). The human was blessed to be made in the image and likeness of God.

We do not know precisely in what way we image God. We do not know whether it is a physical trait, a particular faculty, a spiritual trait, a capacity to do something, or whether the image of God is a constellation of characteristics. The Bible never defines what the *imago Dei*, the image of God, *is*.[5] Of significance to us is that whatever dignity accrues to human beings as a result of this imprint, it is something that only God confers upon us, and that this dignity has been conferred upon us all. This affirmation also implies that there is a certain sanctity that is attached to us insofar as we come from the hands of God and that in some way we have been gifted with God's likeness. This indicates that our humanness as

5 Beverly Eileen Mitchell, Plantations and Death Camps: *Religion, Ideology, and Human Dignity* (Fortress Press, 2009). Although Christian thinkers have speculated as to what the image of God is, they have never denied the significance that the imprint of God bestows upon the human being.

creatures of God, and the glory or sacred worth that derives from our humanness, are not something that we have earned or made ourselves, but come to us as a gift *from* God.[6]

HUMAN DIGNITY IN THE ABRAHAMIC TRADITIONS

My discussion of human dignity has a Jewish–Christian foundation. Muslim scholars share many elements that are consistent with a Jewish and a Christian understanding of human dignity. I have already articulated a Christian foundation for this dignity. What follows are two examples of what both Jewish and Muslim scholars say about human dignity, which is consistent with a Christian view such as I have established above. Those who may wish to formulate a religious foundation for their view of human dignity, but who are not adherents of any of the Abrahamic traditions, may still find resonance with some of my assertions. In viewing what Judaism and Islam say regarding human dignity, there are important commonalities among the three Abrahamic religious traditions worth noting. Regarding concepts such as the "image of God," "inherent dignity," "inherent value," "equality," and dignity as a "gift from God," there is fundamental agreement. Judaism will be addressed first and then Islam.

Rabbi Yechiel Eckstein writes, "One of Judaism's principal affirmations is that man [*sic*] is created 'in the image of God,'

6 Mitchell, *Plantations and Death Camps*, 43–44.

and therefore of inherent dignity and value. That is why man [*sic*] was created in the singular form of Adam and Eve rather than in a community, say the rabbis. For the Bible is trying to teach us that all people stem from the same mold and have the same [common] ancestry; and all are, therefore, equal. Regularly, we reaffirm this concept of the inherent value and equality of all people through such practices as the Sabbath, burial rites, and many more." Further, Rabbi Eckstein states, "Human life is regarded of such inherent value that with the exception of circumstances involving the cardinal sins of idolatry, sexual immorality and murder, we are commanded to transgress the laws of the Torah in order that we may live and affirm life. Moreover, these central Jewish affirmations have been challenged by many over the years, but never as radically as they were in the last century by the Nazis. For them, a Jew's life was of no inherent value."[7]

Another Jewish scholar, Rabbi Heidi Hoover, affirms the value of each person in terms similar to Rabbi Eckstein. Rabbi Hoover writes, "Judaism places high value on the dignity of each person. In Genesis 1:27, we are told that humanity was made in the image of God—*b'tzelem Elohim*. This teaching urges us to recognize every person's equal value and to treat each other with dignity."[8]

7 Rabbi Yechiel Eckstein, "Jewish Concepts: Judaism on the Worth of Every Person," Jewish Virtual Library, accessed February 20, 2025, https://www.jewishvirtuallibrary.org/judaism-on-the-worth-of-every-person.

8 Rabbi Heidi Hoover, "Treat Every Person with Dignity," My Jewish Learning, August 26, 2014, https://www.myjewishlearning.com/rabbis-without-borders/treat-every-person-with-dignity.

As Jewish and Christian voices also maintain, Muslim scholars affirm that, according to the Qur'an, dignity has been bestowed upon humans above that of most of creation. Ṣaḥīḥ al-Bukhārī, a scholar from the late Middle Ages, maintains that Al-Zubayr ibn al-'Awwam reported the following regarding human dignity, expounding from the Qur'an:

> Human dignity is defined as the right of every person to be valued unconditionally. In Islam, this is embodied in the Quranic concept of "Karamah al-Insaan" (human dignity). Every person, regardless of who he/she is, is to be respected and given certain rights. These rights can never be lost or taken away from a human being regardless of his/her actions, religion, orientation or status. Even a criminal has a right to dignity; and also, while being punished. Punishment should not be intended to humiliate, but to reform or discipline.[9]

Mohammad Hashim Kamali, an Afghan scholar, maintains, "The most explicit affirmation of human dignity (*karamah*) in Islam is found in the Qur'anic verse where God Almighty declares: "We have bestowed dignity on the children of Adam ... and conferred upon them special favors above the greater part of Our creation" (Q Al-Isra 17:70). He continues, "this verse is self-evident in its recognition of inherent dignity for all human beings without qualification

9 "The Islamic Concept of Human Dignity," Akhuwat, accessed February 20, 2025, https://akhuwatuk.org/the-islamic-concept-of-dignity. Akhuwat is an organization committed to fighting poverty.

of any kind." The Qur'an commentator Shihab al-Din al-Alusi (d. 1854) thus wrote that, "everyone and all members of the human race, including the pious and the sinner, are endowed with dignity, nobility and honor, which cannot be made exclusive to any particular group or class of people." Kamali maintains,

> Twentieth-century Muslim commentators have also gone on record to say that dignity is not earned by meritorious conduct; it is established as an expression of God's grace as a natural and absolute right of every human person as of the moment of birth. It is God-given, hence, no individual or state may take it away from anyone. As to the question of whether the dignity of a criminal is also recognised—the answer is yes, with the proviso, however, that it is partially compromised to the extent that a court decision on punishment may be enforced, even if punishment involves some erosion of dignity, but beyond that the personal dignity of prisoners must be observed.[10]

This short survey of the Abrahamic traditions regarding human dignity indicates a consensus that it is something *God* confers upon all. Islam makes the explicit point that this bestowal of dignity upon humans is a distinctive feature that elevates them above all other creatures in the good

---

10 Mohammad Hashim Kamali, "Human Dignity in Islam and Its Impact on Society," *New Straits Times*, October 25, 2017, https://www.nst.com.my/opinion/columnists/2017/10/294803/human-dignity-islam-and-its-impact-society.

Creation. There is also a distinction within Islam's discussion of human dignity; that is, human dignity may be "partially compromised" as punishment meted out by a court. Islam, apart from Judaism and Christianity, explicitly links the bestowal of dignity upon human beings, as an expression of divine love.[11]

HUMAN DIGNITY DEFINED

If in some way we image the Creator God, this implies some kind of dignity or glory that surrounds who and what we are and that in some way, we can (and must) recognize that dignity as something of value which warrants that each person be treated with the respect and honor due to any human being. The question of human dignity has received considerable attention in the social sciences, contemporarily; particularly, as more attention has been given to the concept of universal human rights.[12]

I maintain that this dignity is reflective of the stamp of the divine on us as creatures made in the image of God. Like the image of God, this dignity (or glory) is something that only God confers upon us all. This affirmation also implies that there is a certain sanctity that is attached to us insofar

11 I share the Islamic assertion regarding what I call the "graced" dimension of human dignity. We don't lose our dignity, even when we sin, for that dignity is not predicated upon what we do or fail to do.

12 Despite the absence of consensus about the nature of human dignity, I believe it is not only possible, but *necessary* to attempt to sketch an outline of the elements of this dignity for the purpose of our discussion.

as we come from the hand of God and that in some way we have been gifted with God's likeness. This indicates that our humanness as creatures of God, and the glory or sacred worth that derives from our humanness, are not something that we have earned or made ourselves. This dignity is never to be confused with being "dignified."[13]

Human dignity is a decidedly graced aspect of who we are in our creatureliness. It is a gift, and as a gift, it is not something one can earn. It is not connected with what we do or fail to do. It is not related to our conduct. Thus, even those who commit heinous crimes are entitled to the respect that comes by virtue of being human. (Again, this emphasizes the *grace* of our humanness.) Human dignity is given to *all* humans, regardless of abilities, capabilities, or disabilities, physical or mental. This dignity is not mitigated by our economic, social, or political status or gender identity or sexual orientation. This dignity is granted to us from the beginning of life and follows us to the grave.

It is impossible to address the nature of human dignity without addressing the relationship between freedom and dignity. Freedom is a critical component to any notion of human dignity because it affords the human creature the opportunity to realize his or her or their potential as a fully

13 "Dignity" and "dignified" appear related; however, in the context of this discussion the distinction is as sharp as the difference between night and day. "Dignified" is something that we may perform, consciously or subconsciously, that projects that the one who employs it is a figure who commands respect. However, *dignity* is not something we perform nor a role we may play, in certain circumstances.

responsible creature made in the image of God. Freedom is the condition for the possibility of self-governance. Freedom gives us the agency to exercise the right to self-determination. It includes the ability to make choices and decisions about how one will live one's life; and allows one to regulate his or her or their own actions. It involves the right to attempt to achieve personal goals to the best of one's ability without coercion or interference.[14]

Freedom is the essential foundation upon which human beings are equipped to live out their lives in ways that make them answerable to God for the consequences of their actions, choices, and decisions within the human family. With freedom comes great responsibility. Freedom is an essential theological component of what constitutes human dignity. Freedom is the instrument by which, through divine grace, we can obey the double commandment to love God and love our neighbor. The freedom to determine one's destiny, to fulfill one's calling, and to practice the commandment to love God and neighbor has too often been denied or constricted by economic, social, political, and cultural forces, circumscribed by laws enacted, policies made, and rules enshrined in institutions to protect access to resources and sociopolitical power in order to safeguard the ideology of white supremacy. Black people in the United States have been in a fight to the death to have their dignity as fully human

14 This discussion is drawn from Beverly Eileen Mitchell, "The African American Struggle for Human Dignity in Chattel Slavery and Afterwards," in *The Handbook of African American Theology*, ed. Frederick Ware, Antonia Michelle Daymond, and Eric Lewis Williams (T&T Clark, 2019), 9–18.

beings acknowledged, respected, and protected through the times of their enslavement, re-enslavement, and legalized segregation. In the midst of this history of dehumanization, they have been viewed as a despised people. Their history has been punctuated by constant attempts to deny their full personhood. No matter their accomplishments, the preference has been to view them in the way they have been characterized or caricatured as creatures closer to beasts rather than as a people endowed with the same measure of gifts, graces, talents, and capabilities of a creature made in the image of God as every other human being.

Human dignity cannot be destroyed. Because this dignity is God's gift to us, no one can rob us of it. This dignity or glory is ultimately indestructible because it reflects the image of God in us, which is itself indestructible. Of course, human dignity or glory can be obscured, assaulted, violated, or hidden by dehumanization, but our dignity *remains*. Despite the legacy of the degradation that Black men, women, and children lived through during enslavement, and because of indignities their descendants came to know through the continual perpetuation of dehumanization and incessant devaluation of their worth and value through the practice of lynching on pretextual grounds, the system of legalized segregation of Jim Crow, and *de jure* segregation in other regions of the United States, they retained their God-given dignity and their humanness despite the persistent messages from the larger, white-dominated society that their lives counted for very little. Despite some of the sociopolitical gains that Black people fought and died for during the Civil Rights Movement, the white political power structure has surreptitiously circumvented that advancement to first-class citizenship for Blacks by sabotaging efforts to repair the moral harm caused by persistent antipathy toward Blacks. Although the successful election and re-election of the first African American president of the United States appeared to reflect the change that the Black singer Sam Cooke sang about had come, that was not to be.[15] By the second term of President Obama's presidency, amid a backlash of resistance to what the election of the first Black president might have been, there emerged a renewal of the attempts to recapture militarized political control over the Black population with a resurgence of police brutality perpetrated against unarmed Black men, women, and even youth.

THE SOCIAL DIMENSION OF HUMAN DIGNITY

Because sociality is a constitutive element of our humanness, there is a social dimension to human dignity. This social dimension is marked by the human need to have our personhood acknowledged or affirmed. This social dimension has an ethical basis. For a sense of well-being, we must respect the dignity of others, as we would want our own dignity respected. This need for reciprocity or mutuality

15 Sam Cooke, "A Change Is Gonna Come," RCA Victor, 1964.

of acknowledgment is so powerful that when it is denied, it increases our suffering.[16] The social dimension of dignity reflects that our humanness is tied to that of every other human being. It means that our humanness is completed in the presence of, or the encounter with, others who also recognize our value and worth as human beings. When we lose sight of our value and worth or that of others, it is easy to treat others as less than human.

Slave narratives indicate that what made the hardships of the enslaved more difficult to bear was that they were not treated as the fully human beings they were. Their dignity was neither acknowledged nor affirmed. In the midst of brutality and multiple deprivations, the lack of regard for their humanness, simply because of their darker hue, *heightened* their experience of suffering, beyond the physical suffering they may have endured. Samuel Ringgold Ward was a fugitive slave from Maryland who became a leader in the Black abolitionist movement and a Christian minister in the nineteenth century. He wrote a memoir in which he makes clear his belief in how deleterious racism was for the enslaved. In that system, by definition, one of the major things that made enslavement such a heinous institution was that the enslaved person was not treated as a genuine human being, with the attendant gifts and graces granted to all others because they were made in the image of God. Ward wrote:

---

16 Raimond Gaita, *A Common Humanity: Thinking About Love and Justice* (Routledge, 2002), xx, 82.

> The enemies of the Negro [*sic*] deny his capacity for improvement or progress; they say he is deficient in morals, manners, intellect, and character. Upon that assertion they base the American doctrine, proclaimed with all the effrontery, that the Negro is neither fit for nor entitled to the rights, immunities and privileges, which the same parties say belong naturally to all men; indeed, some of them go so far as to deny that the Negro belongs to the human family.[17]

Moral philosopher Raimond Gaita captures well this aspect of the social dimension of human dignity. Gaita articulates the need for such acknowledgment of one's dignity in this way: "Treat me as a human being, fully as your equal, without condescension."[18] For Gaita, and I believe rightly so, this assertion is a *justice* issue. Gaita continues this discussion, "It is justice conceived as equality of respect."[19] Further, he maintains that only when one's humanity is fully visible will one be treated as someone who can intelligibly press claims to equal access to goods and opportunities. He applies this discussion of respect for the full humanness of the other, in the context of race or other forms of radical denigration; specifically, for those "who are quite literally treated as less than fully human."[20] The basic starting point for authentic engagement, one-to-one

17 Samuel Ringgold Ward, *Autobiography of a Fugitive Negro* (John Snow, 1855; repr., Wipf & Stock, 2000), 37–38.

18 Gaita, *A Common Humanity*, xx.

19 Gaita, *A Common Humanity*, xx–xxi.

20 Gaita, *A Common Humanity*, xx–xxi.

as individuals or one group to another, is the recognition of another's full humanity. It involves the recognition and respect between one human being and another; an engagement that is authentic, where there is a spirit of mutuality and reciprocity. Without that basic acknowledgment there is no foundation for further interaction. How could there be? Without acknowledgment of the full humanness of another, there are no boundaries; and it is easy to show disrespect, distain, and even contempt. For Gaita, the struggle for social justice (as equality of respect), has important implications for when our systems, institutions, and structure are infected with racism. He contends, "the struggle for social justice, I argue, is the struggle to make our institutions reveal rather than obscure, and then enhance rather than diminish, the full humanity of our fellow citizens."[21] This is a significant point because Gaita goes far beyond an individual focus. In this context, "social" justice involves a moral requirement that extends to social interaction (beyond one-to-one interactions, and includes structures and institutions).

The deliberate, systematic denial of that need for equality of respect exacerbates the experience of any material deprivations one might be forced to suffer. As Gaita writes, "Those who are the victims of injustice suffer not merely certain determinate forms of natural harm—physical or psychological damage, for example—but also the *injustice*

21 Gaita, *A Common Humanity*, xxi.

of their infliction, which is a distinct and irreducible source of torment to them."[22]

The shame we feel when we witness the violation of the dignity of others is the flip side of that social dimension of human dignity. We are quite capable of experiencing repugnance, a sense of horror, and a heaviness of heart in response to the dehumanization of others. The cry of protest of the dehumanized reverberates in our own hearts, if we have empathetic imagination. In turn, in our own souls, *we* can protest the betrayal of that which is sacred in others. That instinctual recoiling from the violent offense against the dignity of a fellow human being testifies to the reality of the presence of the *imago Dei* that resides in all of us and the kinship it brings. Every attempt to deny or obscure it in ourselves and others will leave us feeling *diminished*, if our hearts have not already been hardened.

The reflection of French philosopher Simone Weil seems to convey a similar insight when she writes, "There is in each human being something sacred." She goes on to say, "But it is not his [*sic*] person, which is not anything more than his [*sic*] personality. It is *him* [*sic*], *this* man [*sic*], wholly and simply."[23] Moreover, when articulating what it is that keeps her from putting out a particular person's eyes, she writes, "there is at the very bottom of every human heart something

22 Gaita, *A Common Humanity*, 82, emphasis added.

23 Simone Weil, "What Is Sacred in Every Human Being?," in *Simone Weil: Late Philosophical Writings*, trans., ed., and introd. Eric O. Springsted (University of Notre Dame, 2015), 104, emphasis added.

that goes on expecting, from infancy to the grave, that good and not evil will be done to us, despite the experience of crimes committed, suffered, and observed. This, above all else, is what is sacred in every human being."[24]

It should be clear from this discussion that this concept of human dignity has nothing to do with the way that we human beings may attempt to elevate ourselves in the eyes of fellow human beings, usually at the expense of others. It is closer to the understanding of American writer and Holocaust survivor Terrence Des Pres, who writes that dignity is

> an inward resistance to determination by external forces; a sense of innocence and worth, something to be and untouchable, and which is most vigorous when most threatened—this is a constituent of humanness, one of the irreducible elements of selfhood.[25]

This determination by external forces plagues those who have been consigned to the lower rungs of a racialized hierarchical ladder.

The nature of human dignity as described above is the basis upon which we are able to establish right and just relationships with others, based upon respect for the mark of the divine in each of us. It is the basis upon which we can respond affirmatively to the command to love each other, for

24 Weil, "What Is Sacred in Every Human Being?," 105.

25 Terrence Des Pres, *The Survivor: An Anatomy of Life in the Death Camps* (Oxford University Press, 1976), 197.

example, to love our neighbor as ourselves. This has monumental implications in our sociopolitical life together. In a highly racialized society in which one racial group dominates all others, one cannot expect peace and harmony. The prospect of authentic, mutual engagement with others across racial boundaries is currently negligible. A racialized society foments unrest, which leads to repressive measures which may simulate "peace" when the dust settles. However, domination requires relentless measures of control and ceaseless vigilance on the part of those that dominate to ensure that they retain their power. Racial domination requires a hegemonic reach to ensure that no area of the social order escapes the measures taken to sustain control.

Invariably, those consigned to a lower rung of the racial hierarchy must be rendered defective or deficient to justify the measures taken for social control. The most obvious way to render others defective is through the use of negative stereotypes, vicious caricatures, and blatant lies regarding the character of the racial minority. Non-white racial groups are then viewed as "subhuman" or "inferior." In the eyes of the dominant group, discrimination and even gratuitous violence are now justified. Respect, mutuality, and reciprocity are viewed as unnecessary or even unthinkable in any interaction with those not classified as "white." From the depths of their whole being, African Americans have known instinctively that this racialized mindset and heart-set constitute a diabolical lie that they must resist for their own well-being. As a result of this distorted (mis)understanding of the true nature of our rightful interaction with each other, African Americans have been impelled/compelled to resist their own dehumanization. The rejection of their defacement has shaped the nature of the Black struggle for justice since their involuntary arrival during the Middle Passage.

In a theological conception of human dignity, we acknowledge a basis for a common bond between us. We also have a religious foundation for cultivating a culture of concern for each other. We have grounds for challenging the nature of our economic, social, and political systems which hinder the likelihood of a wholesome life together. As important as it is in a day and time in which some lives are treated as dispensable, we must speak about the dignity that accompanies the human person, especially as we clamor for the protection of human rights.

Yet, even as we dare to speak boldly about the human glory that comes from being made in the image of God, we must also, at the same time, and with the same importance, speak truthfully about the defacement that works to obscure and assault the dignity of others. These two descriptors of the human condition—dignity and defacement—must be held in tension as we articulate further the social and political nature of the sin of defacement. In the next two chapters, I will address the concept of the sin of defacement in terms of its communal and sociopolitical manifestations in the context of white supremacy in the United States. Ultimately, despite defacement and despite attempts to violate it, human dignity, as a reflection of the glory of the *imago Dei*, cannot be destroyed. It is that dimension of us which essentially defines us as human beings. The indestructability of that dignity becomes most clear and obvious when attempts are made to degrade or dehumanize other human beings.

CHAPTER 2

The Sin of Defacement

A WORD ABOUT "SIN"

The term "sin" is a significant theological term, used in Christianity, which refers to things that we think, say, and/or do, that indicate a breach or alienation between God and a human being or groups of human beings; between humans; or an experience of *self*-alienation that reflects an inner conflict within ourselves. The "sin" disrupts relationships between or among each other, but also damages the quality of our relationship with God. Some segments of Christianity use the term freely, frequently, and for just about any action or activity that the individual has deemed "wrong" or "inappropriate" for a follower of Christ to do. They may frame their lives in terms of strict standards of what they consider right or wrong, and they may make such determinations based upon a sacred text or drawn from leaders of one's faith community.

Other segments of Christianity hardly use the term at all. They are unlikely to hear the word from the pulpit. This second group views use of the term as "old-fashioned" or "out of touch with modern times." In a theologically liberal faith community within Christianity, people assume that most people are innately good. These Christians may concede that humans make "mistakes." They may readily acknowledge that even they themselves may sometimes "make poor choices," but they would reject the idea that others and they themselves are *sinful* people. If they give much thought to their standing before God at all, they may believe that they are in pretty good standing with God, who is loving and forgiving.[1]

In the context of my discussion of defacement, I view sin in terms of disruption of relationships in one or more of three major breaches: (1) our relationship with God; (2) our relationship to each other, or (3) our relationship with ourselves (see Matt 22:36–40). I draw my inspiration regarding the connection between sin as a rupture of relationality from theologian Matt Jenson, who asserts, "The sinner is a person who *tries* to *live* without relations, who *lives* as though she had no relations; that is, curved in on herself (*homo*

1 I tend to believe that the repudiation of the concept of sin is often a reaction to the overuse of the term for minor infractions or activities not subject to a moral assessment.

incurvatus in se). The sinner is one who lives as if reality were other than what it is."[2]

Accordingly, I have no qualms about using the word "sin," as I have observed the kind of things that people do to each other, not only in the personal realm, but also within a larger, social context. History is replete with examples that demonstrate the human propensity to do harm to others. With little thought and no remorse, humans frequently deny the full humanity of other groups: gender against gender; one racial group against other racial groups; adherents of one religious tradition against other religious traditions; financially comfortable people showing distain for those who are materially impoverished; and so on.

We need not transgress relationships intentionally to do harm. Insofar as we are imperfect people who do have a propensity to do harm even when we do not want to do so, or fail to do that which we know is right but for various reasons do not act as we should, we need language and terms that describe and convey the various ways in which we transgress against our neighbor.[3] Since this state of affairs is where we are as humans, I believe it is imperative that we bear witness to both the past and the present for wisdom

---

2 Jenson, *The Gravity of Sin*, 191; and reflection on Matt 22: 36–40, the "Double Commandment"; Love of God and Love of Neighbor.

3 The reference to the dilemma in which we fail to do what we know we should do but fail to do so, as well as do that which we know we should not do, is a paraphrase of what the Apostle Paul says about himself in Rom 7:14–25. Out of exasperation he cries, "Wretched person that I am! Who will rescue me from this body of death? Thanks be to God through Jesus Christ our Lord."

that may be applied toward building a better future. In the remainder of this chapter, I will identify and discuss three particular illustrations from our public life in which the term "sin" should be employed.

DEFACEMENT DEFINED

In chapter 1, I discussed at length my notion of human dignity, particularly as it relates to Genesis, chapter 1, which includes the creation of the human. I elaborated on the creation story of the first human, noting that human dignity arises because of God's decision that the human creation would bear the image of God. Insofar as there is some image of the Divine that all humans bear, the human has been *given* sacred worth by God. Drawing from the work of Emmanuel Levinas, whose concept of the Face informs my notion of human dignity, the assault on that dignity by the actions of fellow human beings constitutes what I call "defacement." The Levinasian Face represents the human being, not simply physically, but also intangibly, as articulated in the previous chapter. For Levinas, there is an ethical imperative that humans are commanded to recognize and obey: "Thou shalt not kill" (Exod 20:13). In this imperative, we are confronted with the sacredness of human life; thus, we humans are prohibited from engaging in any action that would violate that proscription.

To Levinas's ethical imperative, I have added an ontological affirmation that testifies to our interconnection with and interdependence on each other as fellow human beings who bear the image of God within them: "You belong to me." These "pronouncements" convey that we are *connected* to each other by virtue of the reality that we, too, bear the image of God, and that this renders us "siblings" in God's family. I maintain that this interconnectedness lays upon us the "holy burden" to care for one another. The significance of our siblinghood, which signifies theologically familial relatedness, is affirmed in the second part of the double commandment: "Love thy neighbor as thyself" (Matt 22:37–39). Love of neighbor in this context forces us to go beyond our "natural" familial kinship. If we engage each other by the commandment of love—even toward our enemies—surely it is imperative that we love *beyond* our racial/ethnic "tribe" or other group affinities. As people, as members of a society, as members of the global community, we cannot expect to live in genuine peace without the praxis of love which, in turn, allows for justice. Otherwise, we will live in a state of perpetual enmity with this person or that person; this group or that group; or these people or those people. If we think that we can live among other people with no regard for their well-being, but only our own, then communally, we will not know peace.[4]

4 Parenthetically, those who profess to be disciples of Christ are frequently reminded of their obligation to those we encounter. However, insofar as white supremacy (expressed as racism) has been and continues to be a governing influence not only in the wider society, but also *within* faith communities in the United States, Christians are left trying to hold in tandem a profession of faith in Christ and, at the same time, live by an apparently stronger allegiance to the ideology of white supremacy than the gospel of

Jewish philosopher Simone Weil maintains that a plea resides deep within every human being that evil should not be done to us. Yet, evil does befall us at one time or another. Unable to shield ourselves from all the evil that may befall us, she maintains that we live with the unending hope that evil will do no harm to us. However, when evil does befall us, there is the inner cry of protest against it. We may not fully understand from where this evil comes. But we are bound to experience profound bewilderment when evil does come to us at the hands of other human beings; nevertheless, that cry of protest will always be there. For Weil, the plea is a prayer to God, as illustrated in the Lord's Prayer, "Lead us not into temptation, and deliver us from evil" (Matt 6:13).[5] Weil, like Levinas, maintains that when a person encounters another human being, there is something compelling within us that is drawn to that person, unless we close ourselves off from others and thwart our empathetic imagination.

Therefore, any violation of the command not to kill or the refusal or inability to acknowledge our interconnectedness to each other reflects *defacement*. The uncoupling of the prefix "de" signifies the marring of the Face, as one might mar a painting or sculpture or statue. To deface a painting or a sculpture or to spoil a wooden carving with a nasty scratch

---

peace. Because ideologies function in ways that deliberately distort or hide the truth of our commitments from us, we are subject to self-delusion. This is why some find it difficult to "process" that we are incapable of perceiving that racism is antithetical to the Gospel imperative, which is governed by the double commandment to love God and to love our neighbor.

5 Simone Weil, "What Is Sacred in Every Human Being," 124.

is to damage, disfigure, or mutilate the work of an artist. When someone assaults the dignity of another human being, that person defaces the dignity of the other; and such actions transgress the law of love. We cannot obliterate the dignity of a fellow human being. However, it is painfully true that we can *assault* or violate that dignity. Unfortunately, we humans have devised a myriad of ways to deface others, individually and communally. In our petty skirmishes with each other, our hateful interactions toward others, or our indifferences toward each other, we find it difficult to embody love of one another. In our capacity to kill others deliberately or the indiscriminate killing of others across international lines, for example war, we seem to look for more ways to deface the dignity of others. Sadly, our dignity can be obscured or profoundly wounded. Nevertheless, the sacred worth gifted to each of us is present when we are born and follows us to our graves. Defacement can help to elucidate the relationship of sin to human dignity. Simply put, the sin of defacement is the assault on the dignity of another. To deface someone or a group is to deny them the respect and honor due to them by virtue of their full humanity. It is to fail to see their sacredness. It is to dismiss a person or persons as having no value or worth. Defacement says that a person does or persons do not matter; that they have no place in the world. It is an attempt to erase the value of their embodied presence and is a challenge to their right to exist.

There is a huge range of acts which could easily be classified as defacement, extending from the humiliating snub of being treated as invisible by the clerk in a store to genocide. Individually or personally, we commit defacement when we render people invisible or inconsequential. It can happen when we avoid truly *perceiving* one another as human as we are, or when we barely acknowledge others' existence. Defacement is also communal, when our communities engage in activities that exclude other racial and ethnic groups from the advantages of a decent life by denying them access to basic human needs—a living wage, the benefits of safe neighborhoods and quality schools, affordable healthcare, and so on—which activities are the features of structural racism. Structural racism is at work when it becomes embedded in legislation, social policies, and cultural practices and customs, which make it legal and the "natural order" of things to keep minoritized groups from the opportunities they need to participate fully in our national life together. The sin of defacement is probably most visible when we question the right of others to exist, especially in "our" spaces.

Although mass deaths are dramatic and horrifying to contemplate, such deaths are not the only measure of suffering of disinherited peoples. Patterns of social abuse can be as devastating to those who experience them. Police brutality seems almost banal in the context of urban living. But the parade of all-too-common killings of unarmed Black people in the last decade cries out for a solution to law enforcement practices that do not see the humanity of the people they approach nor the ones they apprehend. Overly militarized police officers in the neighborhoods of people of color, disrespect in the way "suspects" are approached; assumed guilty before an investigation of the facts, and sending a dragnet into Black neighborhoods to roust Black males indiscriminately while looking for a suspect based upon vague descriptions of a perpetrator are not unheard of in such communities. It is neither paranoid nor conspiratorial to inquire as to whether such law enforcement tactics are practiced in white neighborhoods. The degree to which unacknowledged bias plays a role in police (mis)conduct and operating out of stereotypes deeply ingrained goes unchallenged.

George Floyd was not the only example of police brutality run amok. However, for some reason, his death out of the number of deaths of Black males, Black females, and even children since 2012 garnered sufficient attention to launch massive protests in cities across the United States (and all over the world). Floyd made mistakes in his life, which he freely acknowledged. The out-pouring of response to his death at a particular historical moment functioned as a mirror for Americans to see that what had happened in the past, is happening in the present, and undoubtedly will happen in the foreseeable future without substantive change. For some African Americans, myself included, the killing of Floyd was a triggering event in which we witnessed over and over again (through the marvels of technology,) the unguarded violence perpetrated against yet another Black man. Defacement is not limited to hapless individuals; it happens to communities.

THE PROBLEMATIZED EXISTENCE OF PEOPLE OF COLOR

One important example of defacement which has long troubled me is being reminded in American history about the times when the existence of members of a racialized group has been labeled a "problem." After the Civil War, Black people were dubbed "the Negro problem" (1865), once whites could no longer legally exploit Black people economically as systematically as they had been during enslavement. Afraid of what was to be done with four million *free* Blacks, the "Negro" was now a problem. With the failure to complete Reconstruction after the Civil War, the South determined that it would never again lose control of the Black population. After Reconstruction the first iteration of the domestic terroristic group, the Ku Klux Klan, emerged as Federal troops pulled out of the South. No longer protected by federal troops, Black people were rendered vulnerable to the violence unleashed to keep Southern Blacks under control. Subsequently, the practice of lynching mostly Black men, but also Black women, became a tool to keep Black people "in line." By the end of the nineteenth century came legalized separation of Blacks and whites as another effort at control, which was not successfully challenged until the mid-1950s, and the birth of the Civil Rights Movement.

There has also been "the Indian problem," which referred to Native Americans, who were already in what would become the United States well before they were "discovered" by European settlers, who promptly began to appropriate the land. These "Indians" were sitting on fertile land with a seemingly endless supply of animals in North America. Viewed as obstacles, they were ejected from *their* land; and those who resisted were maltreated and/or victimized through genocide before they were finally forced into "reservations" without "integration" via citizenship. Treaties continued to be made through the mid-1800s, though there was movement away from making them during the nineteenth century. Treaties had often been used as a means of displacing Native Americans and were frequently broken. As the United States moved away from making such treaties, officials determined that the best solution to the problem was to defeat Native Americans in wars, exile them from territory that white settlers coveted, and settle them within the Upper Midwest states or remote western areas without whites around.[6]

Problematized populations did not end with Black people and Native Americans. There was also the "the Chinese problem" (1850s), as well as "the Japanese problem" (1868). In the 1850s, Chinese workers migrated to the United States to work in the gold mines, but also to take on farming and factory work. This meant competition with US workers and threatened to create headaches between the United States and China, especially when Chinese laborers grew successful

6 "The Indians at the Time of Contact, 1600–1850," Library of Congress, accessed February 27, 2025, https://tinyurl.com/muymc. Also see "Permanent Indian Frontier," National Park Service, accessed February 27, 2025, https://www.nps.gov/articles/pifront.htm.

in the United States. The immigration of Chinese workers created economic concerns and racial tensions. It was these tensions that prompted the passage of the Chinese Exclusion Act (1882). Provisions included a ten-year ban on Chinese laborers immigrating to the United States. This Act became the first significant law to restrict immigration into the United States.[7]

The Japanese were the second problematic Asian group for the United States. Because of poor economic conditions in Japan in the 1860s, an influx of Japanese workers immigrated to Hawaii, which had large sugar cane plantations that were labor intensive. Although it would be nearly a hundred years before Hawaii became the fiftieth state of the United States, the immigration of Japanese workers and other ethnic groups already laboring in Hawaii to the mainland caused whites to become more concerned with growing numbers of laborers from other countries, especially Japan. Racial conflicts were developing and concern over the possibility of Japanese expansion militarily. As early as 1906 the United States and Japanese governments forged a "Gentlemen's Agreement" to curtail Japanese immigration. The subsequent Johnson Reed Immigration Quota Act (Immigration Act of 1924) barred anyone who was ineligible for citizenship based on their race or nationality from entering the United States. The law limited the number of immigrants allowed entry into the United States through a national origins quota, and it completely excluded

7 "Chinese Exclusion Act 1882," National Archives, Milestone Documents, accessed March 30, 2025, https://tinyurl.com/hj486c6n.

immigrants from Asia. This effectively ended Japanese immigration to the United States. In all of its parts, the most basic purpose of the 1924 Immigration Act was to preserve the ideal of US homogeneity of the United States.[8]

Subsequently, there was also "the Mexican problem" in the United States in the early 1900s. What was said about "Mexicans" at the turn of the twentieth century—that they were "undesirables"—is much the same as what is being said by those speaking 120 years later. In the early decades of the twentieth century, Mexico itself was perceived as "politically, economically, and culturally backward."[9] The same sentiment is shared by a sizeable number of Americans in the second decade of the twenty-first century. Since Mexico is "backward," it stands to reason that Mexican people from there are "backward," and thus, they are viewed as undesirable and unfit to live in the United States. In the current debates about undocumented immigrants from Latin America, they are described now as "hordes invading the southern border of the United States." Prominent political leaders have characterized the undocumented as "gang members, drug dealers, and rapists." No less desirable are those who are not gang members

8 "The Immigration Act of 1924 (The Johnson-Reed Act)," Office of the Historian, accessed February 27, 2025, https://history.state.gov/milestones/1921-1936/immigration-act.

9 "Mexico itself was perceived as "politically, economically, and culturally backward." Two scholars address this view of Mexico: Erica Blakemore, "The Long History of Anti-Latino-Discrimination in America." https://www.history.com/articles/the-brutal-history-of-anti-latino-discrimination-in-america, accessed 5/2/2025. Michael Burchett, "Latino Stereotypes." Ebsco.com/research-starters-starters/law/latino-stereotypes, 2023, accessed 5/2/2025.

and other troublemakers. They are viewed as here either to live off the largesse of the US government, or, if they are seeking employment, they are here to take ""Black jobs" from Black people and "Hispanic jobs" from Hispanic people.[10] What is not openly voiced in this diatribe is that the Latin Americans are perceived as non-white; thus race is certainly the subtext of their undesirability in some segments of the United States. During his first term as the forty-fifth president of the United States, it was reported that Mr. Trump wondered aloud among his advisers why it was that the United States would accept more immigrants from Haiti, El Salvador, and African countries, nations he described as "s**thole" countries. He also inquired as to why the United States doesn't attract more people from countries such as Norway.[11]

More than one hundred years ago, W. E. B. Dubois addressed the problematic existence of Black people in his short essay, "The Souls of Black Folk":

> To have your right to exist called into question is an act of defacement of the entire collective. Between me and the other world there is ever an unasked question: unasked by some through feelings of delicacy; by others through the difficulty of rightly framing it. All, nevertheless, flutter round it. They approach me in a half-hesitant sort of way, eye me curiously or compassionately, and then, instead of saying directly, How

---

10 See Matt Brown, "Trump's Debate References to 'Black Jobs' and 'Hispanic Jobs' Stir Democratic Anger," *Associated Press*, June 28, 2024.

11 Josh Dawsey, "Trump Derides Protections for Immigrants from 'Shithole' Countries," *The Washington Post*, January 12, 2018.

> does it feel to be a problem? they say, I know an excellent colored man in my town; or, I fought at Mechanicsville; or, Do not these Southern outrages make your blood boil? At these I smile, or am interested, or reduce the boiling to a simmer, as the occasion may require. To the real question, How does it feel to be a problem? I answer seldom a word. [12]

To have one's existence questioned denies one's sacred worth. It says that as a human specimen one is perceived as having no value. That is a serious example of what I mean by "defacement." But defacement is not only an individual act person-to-person. *Groups* exclude groups from full participation in a community or in society, which is an act of defacement of an *entire* collective.

Richard Wright repeated the question of the problematized existence of Negro, but had a different response. It was forthright, straightforward, and to the point. "We don't have a 'Negro' problem. We have a *white* problem" (emphasis added). [13] A contemporary voice, James Baldwin, responded to the offensive question. For him, it was quite clear in *his* mind that the problem lay with the questioner. Baldwin went even further than Wright. The former told his listeners that

---

12 W. E. B. Dubois, *The Souls of Black Folks* (A. C. McClurg, 1903), chap. 2.

13 George Lipsitz retells the response that Richard Wright gave to a French reporter, regarding the "Negro Problem," shortly after World War II. See George Lipsitz, *The Possessive Investment in Whiteness, How White People Profit from Identity Politics*, rev. and expanded ed. (Temple University Press, 2006), 1, emphasis added.

white Americans ought to examine themselves to ascertain the answer as to why they *needed* "the nigger." [14]

His point was that whites have imagined in their own minds who Black people are at the core of their inner being. In reality, at the center of who Black people *really* are is not the image of who or what *whites* say Black people are, for whites have no intimate knowledge of this. They have *imagined* the "Negro" and then created the "Negro," unaware of what they have conjured up in their own minds.

In an interview in which the topic of race came up, Toni Morrison, the prominent Black female author raised in the South, and who went on to write books and teach regarding her encounters with racism, made this astute observation, as she silently thought about her experiences of racism over the years:

> The people who do this thing, who practice racism, are bereft. There is something distorted about the psyche. It's a huge corruption and a distortion. It's like it's a profound neurosis that nobody examines for what it is. It has a deleterious effect on white people, and possibly equal as it is to black people. But when you take it away; when you take away your race, what are you? What are you without racism? Here you are, all strung out, and all you got is your little self. And what is that? Are you any good?

---

14 James Baldwin is quoted as making this assertion that (white) America has created the "nigger" and that they must examine themselves as to why they have done so; apparently, they need the "nigger" and must come to understand why they have that need. This exchange came as a result of Baldwin's interview with Kenneth Clark on May 24, 1963, https://amara.org/videos/EDNtPBD1Yzfv/en/2256905/m. James Baldwin used the word "nigger" unapologetically. I believe the term he used should be quoted as he said it.

> Are you still strong? Are you still smart? Still like yourself? If you can only be tall because someone is on their knees, then you have a serious problem. And my thinking is that white people have a very, very serious problem. They should start thinking about what they can do about it. Take me out of it. [15]

The significant observation I would make is that all four Black writers, who were prominent in the twentieth century (though Morrison, younger than the other three, continued to write into the early decades of the twenty-first century), understood race as a "social construct" whose impact on Black people, but also white people, was troubled by the ideology of white supremacy. These four writers (correctly, I contend) turned the usual framing of the discussion of racism as a *Black* people's problem, spoken of as if racism was *their* problem to solve. All four of them declined to accept responsibility for the origins and perpetuation of racism. It is *white* people, not Black people, that have the problem. The ideology of white supremacy that is expressed through racism serves a significant role in maintaining white dominance and power. Morrison's diagnosis of racism not only put the onus of responsibility squarely where it belongs, but even more, she is clear regarding what it represents spiritually, although she never specifically speaks of the phenomenon in religious terms. It is a distortion of

15 A partial transcription of an interview with author Toni Morrison by journalist Charlie Rose, which took place on May 7, 1993, can be found at https://charlierose.com/videos/18778.

who Black people are: fully human beings. The distortion of Blacks as less than human has a poisonous effect on interrelations across racial lines. Because racism distorts white identity as well. Because the problem of race is a significant obstacle between interrelated "siblings" in the family of God, white supremacy expressed as racism is a profoundly religious problem.

If race is a "social construct," when we truly know who we are, the notion of "race" has no concrete reality, nor any substance to it. While within the social arena, humans impute meaning to the notion that there is such a thing as "race," when we do so, we are living out of an alternate reality that has no basis or power other than that which we abdicate to it. The "race" problem is one of the making of the dominant race that needs it. At times in our country, the existence of particular non-white groups has been perceived as a problem. It is not Blacks or Indigenous peoples or Mexicans or Japanese or Chinese that are the problem. If the very existence of non-whites has often been problematized, if there is a group that sees the existence of everyone else as problematic, this cries out for turning the spotlight on the *real* problem. The real problem is the dominant group that sees everyone *else* as "a problem." This nation is currently (2025) undergoing a renewed concern about undocumented immigrants from Latin America and a renewed interest in using punitive measures to return these "undesirables" to their native countries. There is a recurring theme, when speaking of "problematized" populations, of fear that they will take jobs from the "deserving" (read: whites) and they "contribute" nothing, but cost Americans a pretty penny to live off "hardworking Americans."

Howard Thurman recalls (and repeatedly relays in more than one of his books) an experience where he, as a Black man, was perceived to have transgressed the rules of segregation prior to the Civil Rights Movement by appearing in a "white space." On a trip from Chicago to Memphis, he boarded the last car of the train. He took a seat opposite a white woman whose facial expression betrayed how disturbed she was by the presence of Thurman. When the conductor came through to collect tickets, he took Thurman's first. The conductor then turned to the woman, who asked the conductor, "What is *that* doing in this car?" The conductor responded immediately. He said to her, "*That* has a ticket." Once she found that she could not engage the conductor in discussion about Thurman's presence, she approached others about the outrage she felt. She went on to announce to anyone within the sound of her voice that in Mississippi his presence in the same car as whites would *not* have been tolerated.[16] Racism was *her* problem. This story reveals for the modern reader how ridiculous racism is if one views it with unveiled eyes.

In the history of people of color in what became the United States, defacement has often been a rather violent expression of sin. In this case, the violent expression of defacement is not

16 Howard Thurman, *The Luminous Darkness* (Harper & Row, 1999), 68.

simply the sin of individuals (though these expressions of sin are highly problematic); rather, it is the communal, collective expression of sin that is so corrosive in the long run. This collective, communal expression of sin is structural in nature. It goes beyond individuals. Structural sin becomes embedded by individual decisions that affect all of those who participate in how an institution functions. In turn, the structural expressions of the collective impact those who are part of the institution. So, there is a dynamic, dialectic influence between those who are part of the institution. Structural sin invariably takes on a life of its own. The latter expression of sin as communal or structural is sometimes rejected because the concept of communal sin is viewed as something that does not really exist; sin is something that only *individuals* do. Unfortunately, those who reject the notion of communal or structural sin insist upon viewing sin as an individual phenomenon alone. As long as their latent sin is hidden from them, they need not give racism much thought.

For African Americans, the history of our presence in the United States has been a centuries-long struggle that persists even in the second decade of the twenty-first century. As a people, we suffered through a particularly brutal expression of slavery. The intention was to make the Atlantic Slave trade a permanent fixture of a group of colonies—particularly in the South—because it was economically lucrative. Among the myths that powerful Southern whites fostered was the idea that Africans were uniquely suited, even created, just for the purpose of being used and treated as beasts of burden, forced to work from sun up to sundown, for the enrichment of settlers from Europe who opted to choose the color code, "white," and who would occupy the top rung of the racial hierarchy that they established.

Those who were able to identify as "white" were those who had garnered sociopolitical power to dominate and classify non-whites. Of course, the further one was from the top rung, the lower one's status would be. Superficial differences in appearances could not be understood as a benign expression of the variety of features within the family of God. Instead, these differences were invariably and automatically interpreted as inferior in the eyes of those with the power to impose their will. It was not by accident or happenstance that those with the darker hue and other physiological markers—for example, hair texture, features such as the shape of body types, the shape of the eyes, the size of the nose, the degree to which one's lips were fuller than others—would be consigned to the lowest rung of the racial hierarchy, employed by those who have embraced the claim of superiority, grabbed the resources meant for all, and exercised the power to dominate at any cost.[17]

17 In contemporary scholarship there is growing rejection of the "Black and white" racial binary, which is assumed to exclude other races and ethnicities; therefore, the Black–white binary is not useful for theorizing race for those who are neither Black nor white. I reject this idea. It is unrealistic to expect that race theorists and scholars must always include all other racial groups by engaging their scholarship and discourse in order to be constructive and relevant in addressing issues of race. While I believe that it is vital for all of us to invite, include, and engage other races and ethnicities (or combinations, thereof) in venues of discourse and other ways of engaging others, I maintain that there is still knowledge that arises from

At every stage of our history in the United States, we have been in a fierce battle not only for sociopolitical and economic freedom, but also for the acknowledgment of our dignity as full-fledged members of the human race. Whether it was Reconstruction, lynching, segregation, or other conditions, Black people have had to live in environments where we have been disrespected as fully human beings, with the gifts, graces, foibles, and missed opportunities of every other human being made in the image of God. Despite attempts to remedy three hundred years of enslavement, Black people also had inflicted upon them another one hundred years of spirit-murdering segregation.[18] The granting of rights on one hand, subtle thefts of rights on the other hand, and the denuding of civil rights, made it difficult to live into the promises of the Reconstruction amendments.[19] At every turn, the dominant racial group adopted dozens of measures to ensure that minority populations lost their voting

---

the Black and white binary and it remains a viable category to continue to examine as we address the issue of race. The binary speaks to the extremes of the racial hierarchy; for Black people remain the quintessential non-white. As "quintessential non-whites," their fate foreshadows the experiences of other non-white races. As the fate of those who are at the very bottom of the racial hierarchy, so goes the fate of various groups *classified* as non-whites.

18 The term "spirit-murdering" is borrowed from Patricia Williams, "Spirit-Murdering the Messenger: The Discourse of Finger-Pointing as the Law's Response to Racism," *University of Miami Law Review* 42, no. 1 (1987), at https://repository.law.miami.edu/umlr/vol42/iss1/8.

19 The "Reconstruction Amendments" refer to the 13th which called for the abolition of slavery; the 14th provides for equal protection under the law, and maintains that those who are born in the US and those who are naturalized as US citizens of the US; and the 15th Amendment, prohibits the government from denying citizens the right to vote, based upon race, color, or previous status of servitude.

power by intimidation and violence; redistricting and gerrymandering; all tactics intended to dilute the voting power of non-whites. Moreover, the collusion between the housing industry, banking system, and the Federal government made it possible for more whites to attain middle class status and deliberately denied those same opportunities to Black people. The collusion *still* keeps cities and suburbs nearly as racially segregated as neighborhoods were in the middle to last decades of the twentieth century continues into the third decade of the twenty-first century. Such tactics have been employed to maintain white supremacy. These are measures that keep people historically designated as "inferior," at the bottom rung of the racial hierarchy. The stereotypes of Black men and women arose from the need to view them as having little to offer. They are said to be "lazy," "unintelligent," with "innate criminal propensities," and "overactive libidos." Because of these biases, in the eyes of the dominant culture, Black people are as undeserving as ever.

One might say that these are "old" stereotypes, that perhaps people used to say such things in polite company, but these stereotypes are not used any more. Such stereotypes arose when the economic system of the United States was heavily dependent upon enslavement of those of African descent. One had to manufacture a narrative that justified enslavement, as some people from the Northern states began to question the morality of enslavement, especially given the religious and sociopolitical hypocrisy of this nation. The problem is that the stereotypes have lingered in the conscious and subconscious minds of members of the dominant culture as, somehow, they continue to feel the need to retain them to justify the continued inequality that bedevils our country in the twenty-first century.

As I mentioned earlier, the huge range of acts which could easily be classified as defacement extends from the humiliating snub of being treated as invisible by the clerk in a store to genocide. Individually or personally, we commit defacement when we render people invisible or inconsequential. It can happen when we avoid truly *perceiving* one another, or when we barely acknowledge others' existence. The sin of defacement can also be communal, when our communities engage in activities that exclude other racial and ethnic groups from the advantages of a decent life by denying them access to basic human needs, a living wage, the benefits of safe neighborhoods, quality schools, affordable healthcare, and so on. With institutions tainted by unimaginative ways of thinking, biased policy-making, and callous indifference, Black women face the highest maternal mortality rate in the United States.[20] Black and Brown people were disproportionately adversely affected by the COVID-19 pandemic in the United States. This reality is one that we all should ponder with alarm and sadness. For those among us who are greatly concerned about making America great again, it starts with how we view (and treat) our fellow human beings.

---

20 Areesha Lodhi, "Why Does the US Have Such a High Maternal-Mortality Rate?," *Al Jazeera*, August 17, 2024, https://www.aljazeera.com/news/2024/8/17/why-does-the-us-have-such-a-high-maternal-mortality-rate.

The sin of defacement becomes embedded in legislation, social policies, cultural practices, and customs, which make it legal and the "natural order" of things to keep minoritized groups from the opportunities they need to participate fully in our national life together. That is how structural racism works! The sin of defacement is probably most visible when we question the right of others to exist; especially in "our" spaces. It is true that African Americans have not been put to death, systematically, within this iteration of white supremacy, as has happened with acts of genocide with other groups or in foreign places, for example, in Germany and Poland, Rwanda, or Darfur. And mass deaths need not always be the final outcome for disinherited peoples. Instead, policing policies, employing convenient biases and operating from stereotypes which have no basis in reality, can turn a "routine" traffic stop, conducted by a police officer, into a fatal event that is destructive to everyone whose lives have been devastated by a senseless tragic outcome.

THE DEFACEMENT OF GEORGE FLOYD

On Monday, May 25, 2020, shortly after 8:00 p.m., in Minneapolis, George Floyd's life was about to come to an end. He walked out of a convenience store and returned to a parked car nearby. He had just had a verbal altercation with a young store clerk, who accused him of using a counterfeit $20 bill to purchase cigarettes. He left the store and walked over to a parked car around the corner from the convenience store. Floyd made mistakes in his life, which he himself freely acknowledged. But earlier that day, he had run into an old friend and they stopped to talk for a moment. He shared with his friend that he really wanted to get his life together for the sake of his young daughter. They parted with hope that they would see each other soon. It was now 8:08 p.m. As Floyd sat in the driver's seat of his car, he was approached by police officers. A police officer asked him to step outside the car. Floyd responded by saying he had not done anything. After approaching the car, one of the officers, pulled out his gun and ordered Floyd to show his hands. (It is not clear why the second officer had ordered Floyd to show his hands.) The police officer and his partner persisted in their attempt to get Floyd to comply with their request. Six minutes later, Floyd, now handcuffed, was led to a police car. Meanwhile, Derek Chauvin had arrived and within five minutes put his hands on Floyd, pulled him out of the car, and placed him on his back while still handcuffed. Then Floyd "actively resisted being handcuffed."

Once handcuffed, though, Floyd became compliant while one of the officers explained he was being arrested for "passing counterfeit currency." At about 8:14 p.m. Floyd "stiffened up, fell to the ground, and told the officers he was claustrophobic," according to the report. During this attempt, at 8:19 p.m., Chauvin pulled Floyd away from the passenger side, causing him to fall to the ground, the report said. He lay there, face down, still in handcuffs. The transcripts of bodycam footage show Floyd said more than twenty times he could not breathe as he was restrained. He was also pleading for his mother and begging "please, please, please." That's when witnesses started to film Floyd, who appeared to be in a distressed state. These moments, captured on multiple mobile phones and shared widely on social media, would prove to be Floyd's last. Floyd kept pleading with Chauvin, "please"; and subsequently called out for his deceased mother. At one point, Floyd gasped: "You're going to kill me, man." "Then stop talking, stop yelling," Chauvin said. For more than nine minutes, Chauvin kept his knees on Floyd's neck, and said, "It takes a heck of a lot of oxygen to talk." Floyd said: "Can't believe this, man. Mom, love you. Love you. Tell my kids I love them. I'm dead." A female bystander told the police: "His nose is bleeding, come on now!" Video footage of the encounter shows at one point Chauvin, with his hands in both pockets, bearing his full weight down on Floyd's head and neck. About six minutes into that period, Floyd became nonresponsive. In videos of the incident, this was when Floyd fell silent, as bystanders urged the officers to check his pulse. One of the officers did just that, checking Floyd's right wrist, but "couldn't find one." Yet the other officers did not move. At 8:27 p.m. Chauvin removed his knees from Floyd's neck. Motionless, Floyd was rolled on to a gurney and taken to the Hennepin County Medical Center in an ambulance. About an hour later, he was pronounced dead.

The unfolding tableau evoked the image of Chauvin as a cowboy who had successfully "roped" Floyd like a wild steer. His dignity was assaulted but not destroyed. It was clear to the crowd that the man was suffering, frightened, and in physical distress. The law enforcement officers saw yet another violator of the law, who disrespected the authority of the police. They were incapable of responding to him as a fellow human being. They never saw him in that light. They never saw themselves in him. The defacement of the other begins within *us.*

CHAPTER 3

A Theological Critique of White Supremacy

> We are unable to really "see" each other as we really are. It is as if we have cataracts covering our eyes because our lenses are "cloudy." Left untreated, we will lose our sight altogether.
>
> Beverly Eileen Mitchell

WHITE SUPREMACY: A PROBLEMATIC IDEA

White supremacy has been tackled in various disciplines as a sociopolitical problem. I am also seeing a fair bit of discussion of the need for political solidarity in the face of white supremacy. However, I remain convinced that, at its core, white supremacy is a profoundly spiritual/religious problem with economic, social, political, and cultural implications. I fear that if we *only* think of cross-racial solidarity in political terms, we place ourselves at a disadvantage in the struggle to resist the grip that white supremacy has on our society. I will begin with a brief discussion of the social context in which racism, race, and the ideology of white supremacy emerged and took root in the British colonies of North America, which came to be known as the United States.

Prior to the sixteenth century, the term "race" was used infrequently; and when it was used, it was a word employed to identify groups of people with a kinship or group connection. Portuguese explorers, led by Prince Henry the Navigator, arrived in West Africa in the early fifteenth century. The Spanish, under the leadership of Christopher Columbus, arrived in the Americas in 1492. The people on both continents were physically, sociopolitically, religiously, and culturally different from the Europeans. In this context, these differences were automatically perceived as signs of inferiority on the part of those who were not European.[1] The modern-day use of the term "race" (identifying groups of people by physical traits, appearance, or characteristics) is a "human" invention; that is, it is not based upon a biological reality. The notion of race as we understand the term today gradually emerged in the British colonies of North America,

1 "Beginnings, Exploration and Colonization," Library of Congress, accessed February 27, 2025, https://tinyurl.com/46v5td7d. Africans came to North, Central, and South America in the early 1500s; some were free and others were enslaved.

as justification for both colonialism and enslavement.[2] Ironically, the notion of white superiority and its embodiment in the ideology of white supremacy has long outlived the economic system it was devised to justify, and has taken on a life of its own.

As Bangstad Sindre and Agustín Fuentes explain, racism is premised on the idea that humanity should be divided into distinct biological groups or "races," and that different "races" stand in a ranked and hierarchical relation to one another. They contend that racism assumes that human "races" are distinctly separate and that there are clear-cut clusters of people which are based upon biological criteria that are fixed and account for their conduct. This notion of a biological reality to race was discredited in the twentieth century.[3] However, Kevin A. Bird, John P. Jackson Jr., and Andrew Winston contend that recent academic journal articles and books are reviving the notion of race as a biological reality. These contemporary "racial hereditarian research" claims derive from modern genetics, such as genome-wide studies, and evolutionary biology.[4]

---

2 "Historical Foundations of Race," National Museum of African American History and Culture, accessed February 27, 2025, https://nmaahc.si.edu/learn/talking-about-race/topics/historical-foundations-race.

3 See "Race and Racism," in *The Open Encyclopedia of Anthropology*, ed. Rachel Cantave, accessed February 27, 2025, https://www.anthroencyclopedia.com/entry/race-and-racism. See also, Kevin A. Bird, John P. Jackson Jr., and Andrew Winston. "Confronting Scientific Racism in Psychology: Lessons from Evolutionary Biology and Genetics," *American Psychologist* 79, no. 4 (2024), 497–508, https://doi.org/10.1037/amp0001228.

4 Bird, Jackson, and Winston, "Confronting Scientific Racism in Psychology," 497.

Those "scientists" who are resurrecting scientific racism contend that the categories of race do offer meaningful ways to categorize diverse human groups. They maintain that evolved genetic differences among populations are "important," for these categories can help to explain *immutable* differences among the categorized groups, such as cognitive ability, educational attainment, crime, sexual behavior, and wealth. Of course, the purpose is the same as it was two hundred years ago: to naturalize inequality. These claims remain a serious source of harm not only by naturalizing inequality, but also by offering "scientific" support for it.[5] This tactic of those wishing to resurrect scientific racism supports Ta-Nehisi Coates's assertion that "Race is the child of racism, *not* the father."[6] Sindre and Fuentes contend that although humans do vary biologically, their variation does not correspond to the racial categories "established" at an earlier historical time.[7] The attempt to find a way to link biology and social engineering demonstrates the degree to which some members of the dominant culture *need* to find

---

5 Bird, Jackson, and Winston, "Confronting Scientific Racism in Psychology."

6 Ta-Nehisi Coates, *Between the World and Me* (Spiegel & Grau, 2015), 7, emphasis added.

7 Scientists who in one way or another espoused views which denigrated the full humanity of those of African descent and gave license to others to uphold the inferiority of those of African descent in the name of "science" include: Henry Home, Lord Kames; Carl Linnaeus; Charles White; Georges-Louis Leclerc, Comte de Buffon; Johann Blumenbach; Benjamin Rush; Christoph Meiners; Georges Cuvier; Franz Ignaz Pruner; Arthur de Gobineau; Pieter Camper; and Samuel A. Cartwright, to name a few.

ways to buttress their belief in their inherent superiority to justify their dominance. Howard Thurman's observation regarding race exposes their underlying insecurity and the lengths that they are willing to go to reassure themselves of the righteousness of their claim:

> The measure of a man's estimate of your strength is the kind of weapons he feels that he must use in order to hold you fast in a prescribed place.[8]

The ideology of white supremacy is a *systems*-based expression of what is commonly referred to as "racism." The essential idea of the ideology of white supremacy is that whites are the superior race; consequently, this self-defined status among all other races (and ethnicities) is perceived by whites as having granted them the right to hoard available resources and exercise the sociopolitical power that satisfies their will-to-power. In a racial hierarchy, whereby one group has designated itself as superior, those who are classified as other than white are likely to be viewed as members of an inferior race, and appropriately subject to the will of the alleged superior race.

White supremacy is an overarching ideology that covers various expressions of racism, whether we are speaking of racism toward Blacks, Asians and other non-white racial/ethnic groups; racial anti-Semitism (where Jews are perceived as a *race*, not a religious group); racialized anti-Muslim

8 Thurman, *The Luminous Darkness*, 71.

prejudice (where all Muslims are perceived as "Arabs" and Muslims are treated as an inferior *racial* group, not as a culturally diverse religious group); or racialized prejudice against people of Hispanic/Latinx ethnicity—hence, the obsession with immigration from the southern border of the United States in political discourse these days. These virulent forms of social exclusion bear characteristics of racialization that have been imposed on diverse people who are not classified as white. Their perceived traits are negative, stereotypical, innate, and permanent. We can no longer view these forms of exclusion as completely separate phenomena but must also recognize them as *expressions* of white dominance that are interrelated because they are spawned by the same "father" (white supremacy).

The fact that these forms of social exclusion are interrelated offers a *theological* basis upon which diverse religious communities might band together for a common cause. I acknowledge that there is a tendency when speaking of race to frame the discussion of racism in terms of the Black/white binary, as if the problem of race is one confined to Black people and white people alone. For those people of color who are not Black, one might have the impression that racism leaves other races and ethnic groups feeling as though their experiences of racism get very little attention. However, I do assert that anti-Black racism is but one expression of white supremacy.[9] The goal of authentic solidarity

9 I do sympathize with those other racialized minorities. To the extent that I can, I sometimes make connections between the experiences of other

is to collaborate across racialized groups. Without the commitment to solidarity, white supremacy leaves all of us vulnerable. Squabbling or holding hard feelings *between* racialized groups gives ammunition to those who would readily exploit that conflict to sustain white dominance.

Sociologically, an ideology can be understood as the sum total of a person's values, beliefs, assumptions, and expectations which are perceived as providing a plausible explanation regarding how the world works. Psychologist Nicki Lisa Cole maintains that ideologies exist within society, within groups, and between people. They shape peoples' thoughts, actions, and interactions, along with what happens in society.[10]

British literary theorist Terry Eagleton adds to this definition that an ideology is a system of concepts and views which serves to make sense of the world while obscuring the social interests that are expressed in the ideology. For Eagleton, his notion of ideology is a "closed system," wherein this system of thought maintains itself in the face of contradictory or inconsistent experience. (This is often seen in exchanges across racial lines, with a measure of defensiveness that is

racialized communities and my own experience as one Black woman. However, I also maintain that, while familiar to me, I think those from other racialized racial/ethnic groups are better suited to bring a nuanced voice to what I may be missing and address the challenges of white supremacy from their own communities. I see myself as a "co-laborer" with other minoritized groups which struggle for justice.

10 Nicki Lisa Cole, "Theories of Ideology: The Concept and Its Relationship to Marxist Theory," ThoughtCo., July 3, 2019, https://www.thoughtco.com/ideology-definition-3026356.

content to reject *any* position that raises resistance toward their own.)[11]

White supremacy creeps into every corner of our society, into the economic, social, cultural, and political realms. It is reflected in the enforcement of our laws. It is reflected in our criminal justice system. It certainly shapes our economic system. Whoever occupies the top rung of the racial hierarchy can determine the types of jobs to which we have access, the amount of money we can make, where we live, and the schools we attend. White supremacy has even *in*fected our religious lives. It shapes how we view ourselves and how we view others. This is what ideologies do. Whether we acknowledge its presence or not, whether we want to be a part of it or not, we are all entangled in the works of this ideology and, therefore, are implicated. As such, where white supremacy is the reigning ideology operating within our society, there are no "innocent" bystanders.

The challenge of letting go of our conditioned interpretation of what the racial classifications of "white," "Black," "brown," "red," and "yellow" have meant persists because of our conditioning of what those racial classifications mean *within the ideology of white supremacy.* Within this ideology, the racial color code "white" signifies several things: (1) those who are white are innately superior; (2) those coded as "white" represent the "norm" of what it means to be human; (3) because of their innate superiority those

11 Terry Eagleton, *Ideology: An Introduction* (Verso, 1991), as it appears in the previously cited article by Nicki Lisa Cole.

classified as "white" are entitled to the lion's share of all the benefits and resources available within society; and (4) those coded as "white" have all the power necessary to govern and dominate all "inferior" races as they deem fit. It is hard for some groups to let go of the human-devised classification system. (For those who derive some benefit from these classifications, whether physically, spiritually, materially, emotionally, or psychologically, the call to dismantle these racial classifications permanently would provoke great resistance.)

Within the racial color code "Black," several things are signified, as well: (1) those who are "Black" are deemed innately inferior; (2) historically, those coded Black have been variously determined to be deficient, subhuman, a different species from *homo sapiens*; (3) because they are always assumed to be innately inferior, the quality of their lives is determined by the superior race; and (4) "Blacks" are "uniquely" consigned to perpetual servitude. As one can surmise, the "white" and "Black" races represent the extremes of polarity. One cannot have a "white" race without having a "Black" one, and *vice versa*. One "race" dominates (all others), and the Black "race" is necessarily dominated. Between the range of "white" and "Black" races, other "races" have been classified, depending upon whether they are closer in skin tone to "white" or to "Black."

A sticking point relative to the notion of "dismantling" white supremacy is the problem of the tendency to conflate white skin tone and the phenomenon of "whiteness." Even though white supremacy uses skin tone to define the classifications of our racial system, we must learn to distinguish between white skin tone and "whiteness." Our inability or our refusal to do so will allow what I would call a "death-dealing" ideology to justify a social order designed to perpetuate inequality, unjust suffering, and a deformation of our moral character. It will keep us bound to a way of life that makes it impossible to exercise our freedom *for* the support of each other rather than to bind all of us to a perpetual state of insecurity. To critique white supremacy is not to demonize people whose skin color happens to be white; for they too, like we are, are fellow human beings, made in the image of God, and endowed with the dignity that comes from this imaging. Unfortunately, some white people have difficulty in making the distinction between white skin color and the term "whiteness." Whiteness normalizes white racial identity where non-white persons are seen as inferior and/or abnormal. Whiteness racializes the identity of those classified "white;" whereby white customs, culture, and beliefs operate as the standard by which all non-white racialized groups are compared, unfavorably.[12] Consequently, white people *experience* the critique of white supremacy as being anti-white people and/or "racist." This fear is regrettable because that *mis*perception of the critique of white supremacy precludes the kind of consciousness-raising necessary for genuine transformation in our communal life

12 "Whiteness." National Museum of African American History and Culture (NMAACH), accessed February 28, 2025, https://nmaahc.si.edu/learn/talking-about-race/topics/whiteness.

together. I assert emphatically, that *being* a white person or a person with white skin is *not* evil; but clinging to the ideology of white supremacy *is*.

The scholar Hamad Dabashi rightly contends that Europeans are the ones who have racialized others and reserved for themselves, and the settlers of North America and Australia, signifiers of superiority. The historical basis for these color classifications has their origin during the Enlightenment, a period of time in which racist designations came to "full 'scientific' blooming." Racism became the rationale for the color codification of the relation of power and abuse, just as sexism is the gendered codification in which males are designated superior to those codified as "female." Dabashi maintains it remains to be seen how such codification regarding gender will be modified in light of the recently recognized fluidity that renders the male/female binary increasingly irrelevant. Dabashi argues that racism as a color codification of the relation of power and abuse is a by-product of the colonial conquest of the world for economic exploitation.[13]

Dabashi's unveiling of the significance of the assertion that race is a social construction was not lost on Toni Morrison or James Baldwin (among many others historically), for both critiqued "whiteness." [14] In the essay, "On Being

13 See Hamad Dabashi, "White Is Not a Colour—White Is an Ideology," Al Jazeera, July 23, 2021, https://www.aljazeera.com/opinions/2021/7/23/white-is-not-a-colour-white-is-an-ideology. Dabashi is a Professor of Iranian Studies and Comparative Literature at Columbia University.

14 Justin Kirkland, "Toni Morrison Broke Down the Truth About White Supremacy in a Powerful 1993 PBS Interview," *Esquire*, August 6, 2019, https://www.esquire.com/entertainment/books/a28621535/

White and Other Lies," James Baldwin discusses the *choice* to become white when European immigrants reached American shores (emphasis added). People gave up their unique heritages for homogeneity. As he contends, "America became white—the people who, as they claim, "settled" this country became white—because of the necessity of denying the Black presence, and justifying Black subjugation."[15] Baldwin goes on to say, "This led me to question how we see ourselves as Americans today, and the future of race in America because of this homogeny."[16] I do not see a definitive answer to either question.

Writers such as Ta-Nehisi Coates continue to challenge white supremacy and all that comes from the notion of "whiteness." Several high-profile cases, in which unarmed (mostly) men have met an untimely end as a result of a "routine" encounter with law enforcement officers, suggest that we are living in yet another era in which challenging white supremacy requires a renewal of commitment to participate in the struggle for racial justice, *with a sense of urgency.* In his letter to his teenage son, Coates shares wisdom from his own experiences, having grown up in West Baltimore. He speaks

---

toni-morrison-white-supremacy-charlie-rose-interview-racism; Michael Oliver, "James Baldwin and the 'Lie of Whiteness': Toward an Ethic of Culpability, Complicity, and Confession," *Religions* 12, no. 6 (2021), 447, https://doi.org/10.3390/rel12060447.

15 James Baldwin, "On Being White ... and Other Lies," in *The Cross of Redemption, Uncollected Writings*, ed. and introd. Randall Kenan (Vintage Press, 2011), 167.

16 Chloe Miller, "'There Is No White Community': Cultural Appropriation and Pop-Culture in the US," University of Notre Dame, September 4, 2023, https://sites.nd.edu/jamesbaldwin/tag/on-being-white.

matter-of-factly rather than angrily of those who "believe they are white." Again, the term "white" has nothing to do with the color one's skin but rather signifies a condition or state of mind. Those classified as such believe that: (1) whiteness sanctions the idea that whites are superior to those who are not white; and further, that (2) their racial classification authorizes them to dominate and control those who are not white. A case in point is law enforcement personnel and the difference in how they function in neighborhoods of white people. By and large, police officers are sworn "to protect and to serve" in the communities where they are assigned.

However, in distressed neighborhoods that are predominately populated by people of color—especially those who are Black—the residents are both over-policed *and* underserved. Those neighborhoods, with poverty that hinders growth, are likely to curb full participation in civic life. Additionally, these neighborhoods—which suffer from a lack of enough affordable housing, a lack of affordable healthcare, and insufficient funding for a quality education, in addition to experiencing high levels of unemployment or underemployment and of substance abuse of all kinds, a higher crime rate, and lack of investment in the infrastructure—are subject to a much higher rate of police interactions that increase the likelihood that serious injury or death could result.[17]

---

17 Zinzi Bailey, ScD, provided a report to the American Medical Association on structural racism and how it works: "What Is Structural Racism?," Health Equity, accessed February 27, 2025, https://www.ama-assn.org/delivering-care/health-equity/what-structural-racism. Also, the NAACP has a criminal factsheet that reports data regarding the interplay between the

The suggestion that the frequency of incidents of police brutality involving Black people makes it appear that there *is* a war on Black bodies should not be dismissed out of hand. What we have here is an illustration of how structural racism works; how resources are less available in Black communities than they are in white communities. The institutions identified above are part of systems and structures that are dependent upon each other. They are interconnected and each area feeds into the others.

These interrelated systems are subject to unintentional and intentional biases that serve a purpose. Structural racism taints every aspect of our society. Initially, structural racism can appear as though it is "hidden" in plain sight. However, I contend that this "set-up" is intentional, and important sectors of the public know exactly what is going on and participate in it. Our sociopolitical stated ideals do not match what is actually happening day after day. This brings into question the sincerity of our claims that we do embrace the notions of equality and equity. Wherever there are big disparities present within differing racial groups regarding distribution of resources and the difference between whether a racial group is flourishing at the expense of those racial groups that are failing to thrive, we are looking at defacement. We are looking at places and spaces where the love of neighbor does not abound.

Exposing the truth of the notion that white supremacy is a social construct, without empirical reality, can be liberating

---

criminal justice system and structural racism's impact on African American communities, accessed February 27, 2025, https://tinyurl.com/3v94ebyn.

because both those at the top of the racial hierarchy and those who are only "faces at the bottom of the well," can be freed by embracing the truth that these categories have no basis in reality.[18] We are liberated to commit ourselves to respect the honor and worth as human beings no more and no less than anyone else.

Dabashi rightly maintains that too often we mistakenly conflate the designation of "race" with the color of a person's skin.[19] That conflation remains the origin and perpetuation of needless confusion. In reality, the normal diversity among the human population simply indicates that we are not clones of one human being or another. The pseudo-scientific notion that the value and worth of individuals can be determined on the basis of skin tone and other incidental physical features, or that these physical traits reveal the nature of another's character or level of intelligence, or signify the level of a human's value and worth, is nothing short of ludicrous.

Dabashi makes it clear that the word "white" in the context of referring to racism is not a signifier for skin color. In this vital context, "white" functions as an ideology. Only those who think they are entitled to certain privileges that must be denied to others whom they would call "Black," "brown," "red," or "yellow" are truly "white." Since the early modern era, the color code of access to benefits, opportunities, and power, is *white*. Those who are classified as "white" have and

18 The use of the phrase in quotation marks was inspired by the title of a book by Derrick Bell. See Derrick Bell, *Faces at the Bottom of the Well*, rev. ed. (Basic Books, 2018).

19 Dabashi, "White Is Not a Colour."

continue to profit from this fiction. Those who have been classified based upon their darkness of hue tend not to benefit nearly as much as those classified as white. In fact, the darker the hue, the more one is automatically perceived as having far less value or worth than those classified as white. This system of color coding has been employed with great effect to separate whites from persons classified as non-white; and the non-whites are encouraged to squabble with other non-whites. It is noted that not every white person profits from this socioeconomic classification of color. However, there are those whites who, for a variety of reasons, may latch on to their white color, and console themselves with the "promise or possibility" that comes from the status of being "classified as white" and are comforted by whatever they can glean and take comfort from not being classified as a non-white. Mistakenly, they have latched on to their whiteness as designating their superiority over those of a darker hue to the detriment of all. There is only *one* race: human.[20]

In light of Dabashi's discussion, one can safely conclude the following: Our value and worth arises not from how we are classified, but rather from the dignity that God gives to each of us, created in the image of God. No more but certainly no less. Dabashi remains adamant: "There is one true race—the human race—scientifically and anthropologically. The word 'race' is a signifier of racism, it is a coded symbol." "No human being at birth is 'white,' 'black,' 'brown,' 'red,'

20 Dabashi, "White Is Not a Colour."

'yellow' or any other colour," he asserts. Eventually, the infant will be "coded" with the colors that "divide and rule them better." *All* those designated a particular color live in a fiction regarding the centrality of those codified as "white."[21]

Dabashi's unmasking of the color designations of race brings a much-needed clarity that makes possible the deliverance of *all* humans. For racialized populations who did not share in the benefits exacted in a racialized society, they recognize that color functions as a coding for determining which group will benefit the most in terms of access to resources and power. They perceive the unveiling of a fiction devised to justify economic exploitation, and eventually become fully conscious of a deeply ingrained hierarchy around which the lives of persons of color are circumscribed. This awareness is indeed their liberation. For those who have identified with the designation of white, the unraveling of the color fiction may not be welcome news.

Dabashi's analysis of race articulates the conditions for the possibility that the problem of race may no longer plague us. He asserts that being "white" is today an ideological conviction that people acquire as they ignore the full history of this country and are indoctrinated not just into racism but even more basically into what he refers to as "racialized thinking." He further states, "Being 'white' is not a biological predicate by virtue of which one is condemned to hatred and bigotry. No one is." The nasty part of being "white" is, he contends,

21 Dabashi, "White Is Not a Colour."

an ideological conviction in which one is convinced that one is a superior human being. Overcoming the "disease of racism," he maintains, is to begin with the undoing of the social construction of races that is the premise of racism. Dabashi rightly contends that the "long and murderous history of racial hatred" was fully on display during the four years of the first Trump presidency. The latter's recent reelection portends a repeat, at minimum, or an escalation of the racial divisiveness of his last term in office.

As we struggle with dismantling white supremacy as a vital ideology, it is important to remind ourselves that the significance of the emergence of white supremacy during the Enlightenment is that this ideology emerged as a way to offer a justification for the enterprise of colonialism and the practice of enslavement by contending that the "inferior" races were consigned to occupy the lower rungs of the racial hierarchy. The legacy and impact of colonialism in certain regions of the world continues to plague us, but the venture has died. Enslavement officially ended after the Civil War, and although economic exploitation remains an active force globally, it is not what it was in its "heyday." The legacy of the plague of white supremacy is present, and the practices associated with white supremacy have lived on. The "justification" has outlived its original intent. The fact that it remains a formidable force, globally, reveals just how tenacious and stubborn this ideology continues to be. It will not simply disappear nor fade away. The roots of it are too engrained.

Those who self-identify as white and are committed to the ideology of white superiority will do whatever they deem necessary to maintain white dominance. Those who have been consigned to the lowest rung of the racial hierarchical ladder, and those who morally object to this illegitimate dominance, must be aware of the nature of this challenge. The methods we employ will have to be strong enough to defeat it. This awareness should help us to navigate the path we walk with wisdom, always keeping in mind that even those who oppose us are also fellow humans made in the image of God.

So, it should be clear now that the critique of white supremacy does not constitute demonization of people whose skin color happens to be "white," just as it does not devalue those who are persons of color, made in the image of God, and endowed with the dignity that comes from this imaging. In a world of frequent and subhuman devaluation of minoritized people, we must ever reaffirm our collective humanness to counter the bombardment of subtle and not-so-subtle messages that would lead us to believe otherwise. The baseline for constructive engagement is one in which we recognize our interrelatedness as fellow human beings. If we are committed to safeguarding the dignity of other human beings, whether on religious grounds or not, this suggests a willingness to confront unjust social arrangements. Instead of sanctioning injustice overtly and covertly that violates human dignity, basic social interactions, social policies, and the passage of laws protecting human dignity would be governed by a serious attempt to work toward the transformation of how our society functions. Those who make such a commitment are living in a way consistent with the social dimension of our dignity in relation to others.

A THEOLOGICAL CRITIQUE OF A SOCIOLOGICAL PHENOMENON

I find transcendence critical when addressing conflicts, for example, defacement, assault, or humiliation toward other human beings, because we humans are fallible, prone to err, and cannot be fully trusted to do right toward our fellow human beings and even for ourselves. I do not perceive the affirmation of God's transcendence as an affront to my agency or my freedom. I trust God's love, wisdom, mercy, and even God's chastisement. I do not see myself in the same category of being as God. The difference between humans and God is not a difference of degree but a difference in kind. Because of the respect, honor, and love I give to God as my creator, redeemer, and sustainer, I do not think according full allegiance to God robs me of anything. Sole allegiance to God, treating God as the only Being that I worship, I see the prohibition against other "gods" as a gift or example of God's regard for my well-being. I do not view myself as an equal to God. If we humans are enjoined not to have any other gods before us, I have no problem with prohibiting anything that is being given priority over God. Also, I perceive that there are very good reasons to avoid prioritizing all other things, no matter how good, that pale in comparison to God. Also, we are hurt by the things that we elevate above and beyond God. The prohibition against idolatry is an act of love on God's part. Despite these convictions, I struggle and sometimes fail to remain faithful to my convictions.

The First Commandment and Idolatry

White supremacy is a theological problem as much as it is anything else. There are economic, social, cultural, and political dimensions of the ideology of white supremacy. But above all else, it is problematic theologically—and pragmatically. White supremacy is a form of idolatry. As the racism of white supremacy is lived out in personal, communal, and institutionalized settings, it becomes an all-out mechanism for determining how we see ourselves and how we see and relate to all kinds of people. It impacts our decisions about where we will live, who we will or won't marry, who we choose as friends, how we raise and teach our children, the quality of our relationship with others, including that which we call God or that which we worship. Humans were made to be creatures that worship. It may be a deity or deities, it may be a view of our self-image, it may be tangible or intangible, it could be something we designate as "spiritual," or it can be completely material. But we are born to worship something; and are likely to worship a number of things. In fact, the sixteenth-century Reformer John Calvin spoke of our minds as being "factories of idol-making."[22] Clearly, Calvin is suggesting that pretty much anything could occupy a role as an idol in our lives and that having an idol (or several) is not unusual.[23] We may have all kinds of ideas regarding "institutional religion." However, this does not nullify the fact that we are creatures made to worship something or Someone. If we operate from that assumption, then almost anything could be considered an object of worship.

In ancient times, materials such as gold, statues, wood, or stone could be fashioned into an object of worship. These days objects of worship, for example, idols, may be less tangible or concrete; but nevertheless, they function as idols. We give them priority in our lives; our lives may revolve around this object, conviction, ideology, or these persons. It is something or someone in which or in whom we place our trust. The theologian Paul Tillich spoke in terms of that thing which is of "ultimate concern" to us; that which has assumed great importance in our lives.[24] This way of articulating that which constitutes an idol is particularly useful. To speak of something as "ultimate" is to signify that the object or person or ideal assumes paramount importance in our lives. "Ultimate" signifies that which is above all else. It could be wealth or status or

---

22 John Calvin, *Institutes of the Christian Religion*, Book I, XI (The Westminster Press, 1970).

23 Myron McVeigh, "Paul Tillich: Dynamics of Faith," accessed February 27, 2025, https://www.ukessays.com/essays/religion/paul-tillich-dynamics-faith-summary-7239.php.

24 Paul Tillich, *Dynamics of Faith* (Harper & Row, 2001), 1–46.

fame. It could be a career or a goal. Many of us may cling physically, psychologically, or spiritually to more than one idol. The ultimate concern may not be a religious object, but it may *function* as something to which we are dedicated and loyal. It could be a special talent, for example, a talent in art, music, or athletic ability, or that one is highly intelligent. It is not uncommon to have multiple idols. In that case there may be several penultimate things that are of great concern to us; but there is likely to be one out of those "several" which is above the rest. It could be particular relationships or certain roles we may be willing to play to seek fulfillment from this idol. That ultimate concern may be something for which we may be willing to give our whole being. The "ultimacy" of the idol signifies that the object of our "worship" is "above all else." As James Bishop observes of Paul Tillich, "Tillich believes that anything, especially finite things, that is ascribed the status of ultimate concern is elevated to the status of God and therefore becomes idolatrous. Such things constitute the affirmation of something which is not ultimate."[25]

My main argument in this chapter is that white supremacy, expressed as racism, is an ideology which maintains that those who are racially classified as "white" are racially superior to all other classified races; that because of their "superiority," they are rightfully entitled to the lion's share of resources in society, and entitled to the advantages and

25 James Bishop, *Bishop's Encyclopedia of Religion, Society and Philosophy*, accessed February 27, 2025, https://jamesbishopblog.com.

opportunities available in society—above all other racial groups; and that whites are entitled to the bulk of socio-political power. The ideology of white supremacy, with its claims of rightful dominance as the "superior," permeates all levels of society, because this ideology reaches far, wide, and deep; and it functions as a "rival faith," and is a way of structuring all areas of society. Adherents to this form of white supremacy are unwilling (and maybe *unable*) to dismantle or to let go of what has become a full-fledged belief system. It is what those who are classified as white may cling to, count on; and certainly, they are unwilling to surrender the advantages and privileges which go with being classified as "white." The writing of George D. Kelsey is a critical voice in the discussion of racism as a "rival" faith; more accurately, a religious faith.[26]

Injunction to Avoid Idolatry

I have given some account of what could constitute idols in modern time, and idolatry—the act of worship of an idol or idols. There are three biblical texts in particular which set the prohibition of any and all rivals to God as Christians generally affirm. The first instance appears in the book of Exodus. There are ten commandments describing that which God's covenanted people were prohibited from doing. The first commandment reads as follows:

---

26 George Kelsey, *The Christian Understanding of Man* (Wipf & Stock, 2010).

> I am the Lord your God, who brought you out of the land of Egypt, out of the house of slavery; you shall have no other gods before me. You shall not make for yourself an idol, whether in the form of anything that is in heaven above, or that is on the earth beneath, or that is in the water under the earth. You shall not bow down to them or worship them; for I the Lord your God am a jealous God ... (Exod 20:2–5a)

Despite the anthropomorphic language, it is clear that God demanded complete and utter loyalty from the covenanted people. In this passage, there is the recognition that there are likely to be other gods. The community was forbidden to do anything that suggested that they were in any way giving obeisance to anyone or anything other than God. There was no room for divided loyalties.

In two biblical texts from the New Testament, we are confronted with a theological warning regarding the need for a singlemindedness of our commitment to the One who has given us life, redeemed us when we have been faithless, and is there to sustain us to the end. As was the case in the Hebrew Bible, we are enjoined not to give allegiance to anything or anyone else. We are to recognize that we may avoid that which seems to promise us much but will never be able to deliver. We can stand firm against anything that we allow to fool us into believing that there may be something that may seduce us into believing that this "something" seems to promise to be more loving, more powerful, more merciful, or more generous to us than the Divine One. A false god cannot give us what we truly need. Anything other than God cannot satisfy us the way God can.

White supremacy is an ideology that competes with the true God. It is an idol of pretense. It cannot deliver what we are seeking. What it brings may fool us, we may think that occupying a high level in the hierarchy of race is of great value, and that it raises our status sociopolitically. The ways in which those who are classified as "white" balk at, deny, and ultimately refuse to surrender "privilege" or take on a "forgetfulness" of the ways in which the social order advantages some but not others.

> Matthew 6:21 indicates that Jesus told his disciples and a crowd that where their treasure is, there you heart will be. Our "hearts" are where our treasure is. Our treasure is that which we value most. For those who commit themselves to the ideology of white supremacy, this "treasure" is likely to be that which they truly "worship" or value as most important above all else. "Where your treasure is, so will your heart be."
>
> In Matthew 6:24, we are warned that we will have to make a choice as to whom we will worship, "with our soul, heart, and mind." We were never intended to serve multiple divine entities. A divided loyalty makes for confusion and we come to realize that a divided loyalty externally divides us internally, for we are unable to give our all to both. "In practical terms, we cannot serve two masters."

As Jesus explains, we cannot truly function faithfully if our loyalties are divided; neither one has our full attention. We may come to resent the competing tugs on our heart. Again, the admonition against divided loyalty protects *us*. It's a dilemma that gives us less, not more peace. It should be clear that: (1) we are creatures made to worship; we can follow that call to worship God in a manner that recognizes that our allegiance must be to God; (2) we are not equipped to worship, let alone to live, with divided loyalties—particularly if our single-mindedness requires our whole selves. No piece of ourselves can be hidden from God. We can only serve one master; not multiple ones.

Karl Barth's Challenge to the Ideology of National Socialism

The twentieth-century theologian Karl Barth penned an important preliminary statement regarding the task of doing theology. Barth was teaching and writing in Germany when Adolf Hitler came to power in 1933. At the time the university faculty and clergy were civil servants paid by the state. He watched faculty colleagues and clergy capitulate to the demand to be loyal to the ideology of National Socialism. There were Christian church leaders who thought that they could serve two masters, Nazism and the church. Theologically, those who taught in areas such as scripture, theology, ethics, and church history—foundational subjects designed to prepare students to serve the Christian church—did not see that their capitulation to Nazism was a threat to the church.

In his 1934 lecture, "The First Commandment as an Axiom of Theology," Barth acknowledges that he is using the term "axiom" in an unusual way. An axiom of theology is not something that can be "proven." For Barth, this axiom of theology is a commandment that "the church is required to *obey*." The theology of the church must be faithful to God's word. His point in this lecture is that there is a presupposition upon which theology is based.

The campaign to get rid of the Jews in Europe was an example of white supremacy at work, expressed as racial anti-Semitism: the idea of restoring the German people to their former glory as a people following their defeat after World War I. With a dream of ushering in a new age between World War I and World War II, the Nazis were hankering after a blood and soil ideology. In this ideology, the goal was the emergence of a "racially pure" Aryan people; a special relationship between the German people and their land would be fostered. This ideology was used to justify the seizure of land in Eastern Europe and force the expulsion of local populations in favor of ethnic Germans.[27]

"Blood and Soil" was an early Nazi slogan used in Germany to evoke the idea of a pure "Aryan" race and the territory it

27 "Origins of Neo-Nazi and White Supremacist Terms and Symbols: Nazi Racial Ideology," United States Holocaust Memorial Museum, accessed February 27, 2025, https://www.ushmm.org/antisemitism/what-is-antisemitism/origins-of-neo-nazi-and-white-supremacist-terms-and-symbols.

wanted to conquer. The concept was foundational to Nazi ideology and its appeal, though it predates the Nazi regime. "Blood" referred to the goal of a "racially pure" Aryan people. "Soil" evoked a vision of the special relationship between the German people and their land. It was also a tool to justify land seizures in Eastern Europe and the forced expulsion of local populations in favor of ethnic Germans.[28]

The continuing significance of Barth in discussion of idolatry is that he paid attention to the power of propaganda to sway those who were part of the leadership of the church. When others could not perceive the threat of the ideology of National Socialism, which permeated all areas of German life, he could. His university colleagues and religious leaders in the Protestant churches were unable to recognize the danger of coupling Nazi ideology with the Christian gospel. Barth could discern that Nazism functioned as a rival "gospel." He was able to do this because he was attentive to the centrality of Jesus Christ, as attested to in Scripture; and not only that, but that the Word of God was not only to be heard, but also to be *obeyed*. For Barth, the real test of whether one has heard the Word is obedience to what one hears. There is a segment of the theological community that "shudders" at the mention of Barth's name. However, for me, he has much credibility in terms of the way his theological understanding can "detect" idolatrous pretensions in a time

28 "Origins of Neo-Nazi and White Supremacist Terms and Symbols: Blood and Soil," United States Holocaust Memorial Museum, accessed February 27, 2025, https://www.ushmm.org/antisemitism/what-is-antisemitism/origins-of-neo-nazi-and-white-supremacist-terms-and-symbols.

and moment when his theological rivals could not until it was far too late. The inability of some segments of American Protestantism to recognize the theological or religious role of white supremacy in American life signals to me that we are repeating the error of Protestantism in Nazi Germany.[29]

With the first commandment as an axiom, theology does not need to offer "proof" (as one would if one were solving a mathematical problem). The axiom is understood to be a "word to the church," which we are required to obey.[30]

Barth, who takes his cue from the sixteenth-century Protestant Reformer Martin Luther, confirms the significance of the first commandment, "You shall have no other gods before me" (for faithful theological reflection as well as faithful discipleship). Luther interpreted that

---

29 White Protestant churches in which white supremacy expressed as racism, whether explicitly or implicitly, while at the same time expressing a commitment to the gospel of Christ, would seem to embody a lame attempt to hold together "two masters." Karl Barth would argue that "invariably" whatever commitment to Christ would eventually be subsumed under white supremacy. The attempt to hold together the ideology of National Socialism and Christianity was a seminal illustration of that phenomenon for Barth. National Socialism became the "voice" that Protestant churches "obeyed" rather than the "voice" of Christ.

30 Karl Barth, "The First Commandment as an Axiom of Theology," in H. Martin Rumscheidt, *The Way of Theology in Karl Barth, Essays and Comments*, introd. Stephen W. Sykes (Pickwick Publications, 1986), 63–78. See Bradley Gray, "The Gods We Make vs. the God We Need," 1517: Christ for You, January 25, 2022, https://tinyurl.com/5n8t3mwn. In interpreting Barth's lecture, Tyler Been correctly reminds the reader that the biblical text *assumes* that there are other gods. See Tyler Been, "The First Commandment as an Axiom of Christian Preaching," *Covenant, The Living Church (TLC)*, September 26, 2023, https://livingchurch.org/covenant/the-first-commandment-as-an-axiom-of-christian-preaching/#:~:text=Barth%20argues%20that%20this%20).

commandment to mean that God is the God in whom human beings place their trust; in whom they have their faith; from whom they expect to receive what they love; and in whom they seek protection from what they fear. For Barth, God is that One to whom one gives one's whole heart unreservedly. Barth goes on to remind the reader of his essay that Luther went on to say that money and possessions, art, wisdom, power, favor, friendship, and honor could in this sense as equally well be real gods as the idol of the heathen, the saints of the papacy, and last, but not least, our deeds and our moral achievements. Wherever the human heart is, wherever is the foundation of our real ultimate confidence and hope, "the *primum movens*" of our vitality and the basis of the security of our lives, there, also, in all truth, is our God. *This* true God is more than worthy of being worshipped, adored, and glorified by all creation. At the very least, this God to whom we dedicate ourselves has claims upon us, and is the One to whom we give our wholehearted allegiance.[31] Barth contends that, for him, a god is whatever people "hang their hearts" on, "whatever they trust."[32] Barth reminds us that the task of the Christian, in light of whom we must obey and through whom we recognize our condition, is to recognize that for humans, we are vulnerable, apart from grace, because we have a propensity to give allegiance to *everything* other than

31 See also, Martin Luther, "The First Commandment," in *The Large Catechism of Martin Luther*, ed. Henry Eyster Jacobs (The Lutheran Library Publishing Ministry, 2018), 16–22, 69.

32 Barth, "The First Commandment as an Axiom of Theology," 69.

God. The continuing relevance of Barth is that theological and religious communities must be astute and alert to rival ideologies that subtly demand our allegiance, and yet fool us into believing that we *can* in fact serve two or more masters. Important, influential theological figures and religious leaders in high places could not discern that Adolf Hitler was not the return of the Christian Messiah. Barth was one of a very few theologians who recognized *early* (1933) the theological/religious dangers of placing one's faith in a human being who promised to make Germany great again. The failure to "read the signs of the time" led to a great deal of suffering and death.

Paul Tillich was a contemporary of Karl Barth. I find that Tillich's discussion of his well-known concept of the nature of faith as "ultimate concern" captures the strength of what we mean when we try to explain the term "idolatry" in modern terms. In reflecting on the question of what we as human beings value the most, what gives life meaning, whether we have properly ordered our priorities in life, the idea of "ultimate concern" is meaningful as we consider how the ideology of white supremacy functions. White supremacy has not only sociopolitical and economic power, but psychological power as well, for those who subscribe to white supremacy.

As one reflects on the decisions people make as they affiliate with one political party or the other, what issues they perceive as most important, in this season of racial tensions in this post–Barack Obama world, there has been keen resistance to any possibility of change in some of the values of the dominant culture. Here, I am referring to the virulent resistance to immigration of persons of color, a punitive posture toward Black people who have been involved in fatal encounters with law enforcement, and tepid efforts to commit to the transformative work of racial equality. The power of white supremacy to shape interactions across racial lines is one in which there is a lack of empathetic imagination, and a resentment of any attempts to address bad acts of the state and its people, past or present. In photos of protesters from MAGA (Make America Great Again) people supporting Donald Trump, I see the same vehement hatred of those protesting integration in the 1960s. I see the fear of the change in demographics and the resentment regarding some people having to settle for less economically than they believe they deserve. There is an atmosphere of blame toward people of color, who are perceived as being responsible for a change in the way of life of those whites who hoped that they would prosper well above minoritized populations. The loss of faith in the supremacy of the white race reveals an (inappropriate) "ultimate" concern insofar as the ideology of white supremacy, predicated on the assumption of white racial superiority, is a rival "faith" regarding ultimate concern which will never be able to provide the kind of security, sense of self-worth, means of sociopolitical power, access to resources, and intangible advantages not available to persons of color that adherents seek.

White Supremacy as a Violation of the Law of Love

As previously mentioned in chapter 1, the "double commandment" (Matt 22:37–40) states that we are to love God with all our heart, soul, and mind. Additionally, we are to love our neighbor as ourselves. Identification of "the neighbor" is revealed at the end of the parable of the Good Samaritan (Luke 10:25–37), where the notion of neighbor is expanded beyond those of immediate proximity to where we live or even a close relative. The "neighbor" is the one who takes care of a person in need. One cannot truly love God and despise others or refuse to offer aid when needed. White supremacy expressed through racism does not allow for love of other humans as we would love ourselves when it comes to people who do not look like them. Some Americans will never conceive of others, who appear "different" from white Americans, in terms of a "neighbor," or just plain fellow human being.

White Supremacy and Right Relationship with God

It is difficult to see how one can have a "clean" relationship with God if one feels ill-will toward a person or a group. People seem to think that ill-will toward a group is not an issue, that God only cares about interpersonal relationships. In fact, having ill-will toward a group *amplifies*, not obscures, the relational damage. Some of us mistakenly believe that an "impersonal" or indifferent posture toward others excuses us. Instead, it exposes us.

Violation of the Law of Love

We are not told to *like* all people or approve of everything the other does, but the quality of love that we are enjoined to practice affirms the dignity of all. It means doing, not withholding, what one can do. It does not mean indiscriminate approval. It does mean that we must cultivate the *practice* of forbearance and a willingness to overlook minor things and be willing to work on the bigger things, if our hearts are open wide.

Leaving No Room for Love

There is nothing more personally wounding than a closed-off heart toward another person, for when we deny the opportunity to truly know the blessing of love and friendship beyond those who are different from us we miss the joys of mutuality and reciprocity in our human interactions, and we lose out on what could be given or received. When we shut the door of our hearts to keep others out, we miss the opportunity to be a channel of blessing and/or the opportunity for the blessing of friendships based on mutuality and reciprocity.

Closing the Gate to Empathetic Imagination

Instead of the practice of forbearance and empathy, we give way to our baser instincts. Standing in the shoes of others is one of the first things we are taught when we are socialized as children. This presupposes that we recognize the personhood of the other, that we do not assume that the people we encounter are no less human than we are. Empathetic imagination offers us the chance to practice putting ourselves in the place of another. We may not always agree with or readily understand what we have heard, but we can perceive reality from a perspective different from our own. It is yet another opportunity for mutuality through understanding another and being understood by the other person.

The problem of white supremacy, which is incredibly intransigent, will not be resolved by legislation or policies or customs or training or church denominational statements. We have been there and done that while circumventing and subverting what a law of justice might demand. These common responses to racism sound good, but they are inadequate for addressing the reality that white supremacy in all its forms is not about individuals making substantive change. If white supremacy is a structural phenomenon, and it is, it requires *structural* changes.

Human dignity forms the basis of viable cross-racial solidarity, and offers a theo-ethical foundation upon which to deconstruct white supremacy. I say this because at its core we are dealing with an ideology that denies the reality that we are *all* creatures, made in the image of God; and that having been gifted with that image, all of us have been blessed with dignity and have sacred worth that ethically *commands* us to view others—to treat others—as we would want to be viewed or treated. Our sense of well-being as humans requires this from each other for a sense of equilibrium and well-being. Human to human, group to group, the ethical demand remains that we are to give respect and receive it, *indiscriminately*. Otherwise, ultimately, it will not go well for any of us in the long run.

The ideology of white supremacy denies all of this. It denies that by virtue of human dignity, we are all siblings to each other. It sets one race above all others. On the one hand, it claims for itself a monopoly of access to power and the means of what makes for human flourishing. On the other hand, it goes to great lengths to deny these things to those arbitrarily classified as lesser beings within the racial hierarchy. White supremacy fosters god-like pretensions in the hearts and minds of the ones who cling to it. Some of our brothers and sisters are clinging to it for dear life.

White supremacy not only pathologizes, but also homogenizes and erases not only differences within the racial group, but also denies the full complexity of what makes the members of that group fully human. White supremacy characterizes the perceived "racial" differences in a way that is always viewed as innate, immutable, deficient, inferior, and therefore, undesirable. All the while, overt and covert racists can try to gaslight people of color by denying that racism still exists or invalidating their experiences through condescension.

With the burgeoning increase in the population of those who have immigrated, both legally and illegally, from poorer countries in Latin America, the response from states most affected by this immigration has been to adopt tougher anti-immigration laws and punitive measures to try to stifle this trend. The fear, reflected in the rhetoric surrounding debates about immigration, strongly suggests that the underlying concern about the illegal status of some of those who have immigrated here has more to do with the fact that those of Latinx/Hispanic descent have become the fastest growing minority, surpassing that of African Americans. Regarding their racial status, although some of Latinx/Hispanic may prefer to self-identify as "white," the anti-immigrant Americans view Latinx-Hispanic diverse ethnicities as a monolithic block. The discomfort surrounding the demographic shift in which projections suggest that whites will no longer occupy a racial majority status in America is undoubtedly behind the near panic of some whites, which seems to be increasing at a feverous pitch. That demographic change will have enormous consequences for the kind of nation we will become. Perhaps the inevitable population movement will force some change in attitudes regarding white supremacy and notions about race in a positive way can help us manage the challenges we could face in the near future.

I am not optimistic that the passage of time will gradually change attitudes. Given how deep-seated racism is in the United States, I believe that a measure of force may play a role in the degree of transformation needed to make the United States safe for non-white populations.

CHAPTER 4

Impediments to Racial Reconciliation

From chapter 3, it should be clear that white supremacy, expressed as racism, is a destructive social arrangement that loosens the bonds between members of a society using a classification system based upon race. Racial classification by features long established the social order within a highly racialized society such as the United States. Social inequality is built into such a system. As previously noted, within the range of diverse racial populations, those classified as Black were assigned to the lowest rung. For those who embrace God, whom they presume to worship, ruptures of our relations via such an order of hierarchy can hinder the divine-human, human-to-human relations unless an intervention is sought. Whatever state of mind we may be in, we bring the feelings associated with those encounters, for example, enmity, strife, fear, strife, and tension, into our interactions. That is why it is a good idea to prepare ourselves, emotionally, psychologically, and spiritually, when we enter into such engagements. Enmity, tension, and even strife—whatever we may carry with us, regardless of our racial classification—will taint the quality of our relationships across racial lines if the toxicity of interactions is not addressed and resolved in constructive ways.

Those who have internalized oppression from experiences where we are treated as inferior, who have been denied access to opportunities to grow and flourish, who experience turmoil rather than peace because of the distortions that arise from not being able to live comfortably in our own skins, are in need of the inner resources to help us heal from the fallout from race-based incidents that can distort the nature of how we relate (or not) to the God we worship, how we relate to each other, and even how we relate to ourselves. If we do concede that racial strife, resentment, bitterness, rage, or shame are unhealthy not only in individuals but within the body politic as well, then hopefully we will be open to being supported and nurtured by people we trust.

Recognizing the tensions that arise out of cross-racial justice work, we might consider the possibility of mending our relationships by doing what is needed for healing ourselves individually, but also extending ourselves to aid in the healing process between ourselves and others. If so, then the possibility of racial reconciliation could be something that we might seriously entertain should we yield to a process of racial reconciliation. If, as I argue, the problem of white supremacy is spiritual at its core, that would suggest that communities of faith of all traditions *could* be helpful in taking the lead in organizing a broad coalition that could turn the possibility of transformation into a reality.

As we identify where we are in the process of preparing to work on racial reconciliation, there are two critical question for us to consider: *Can the races in the United States be reconciled and live in a state of harmony?* The second critical question to ponder is this: *Do Americans have the political will not only to consider that possibility, but also to make a commitment to work toward such a goal?*

When cross-racial groups gather for the purpose of understanding how racism works and how people who have a desire to engage in justice work can change the minds of those who hold racist views and seem hostile to the idea of people of diverse racial/ethnic identities, they can start to engage each other and abandon beliefs and actions which keep racism going. There are white people who desire and are willing to engage in cross-racial interactions to facilitate a healing and reconciliation process. Those who express a desire are likely to find a number of vehicles to be part of peaceful relations across racial lines and come to this work with a sense that these interrelationships can be viewed as ordinary; or at least not something odd or unusual. (In larger urban areas, people can interact on a number of levels without it being viewed as an anomaly. However, in smaller or rural communities, interacting with others across racial lines might be viewed with some degree of suspicion.)

African Americans have had to pick up the tab in the past whenever there were initiatives which sought to address the kind of turmoil that racism and its handmaiden, segregation, added to their lives. An unnecessary burden and hardship on the lives of Black people came as a result of the US Supreme Court decision Plessy v. Ferguson in 1896, which officially legalized segregation of public conveyances, restaurants, schools, playgrounds, housing, and other facilities. Justice Henry Brown wrote the court's majority opinion, which supported the practice of segregation in principle as long as such facilities were equal in quality (the "separate but equal" doctrine). The problem was that these conveyances and institutions were rarely "equal," and African Americans were always at the losing end of the farce. The Plessy v. Ferguson decision gave legal sanction to segregation. Ninety-eight years later, in 1954, the US Supreme Court decision in Brown v. Board of Education, Topeka, Kansas, overturned the approval of segregation, though this case decision was precipitated specifically by concern over the adverse impact of the inequality of public school education on Black children.

IS IT POSSIBLE TO HAVE THOUGHTFUL, GROWN-UP CONVERSATIONS ABOUT RACE?

On Christmas Eve, 2015, Black philosopher George Yancy penned an open letter to "white people in America," which was published in the *New York Times*. In that letter, which he intended to convey how poisonous the ideology of white supremacy was for persons of color, he sought to appeal to the "better nature" of whites in America, whether they were religious or not. Yancy's message was that this false belief system was a major source of oppression for all people who were classified as *non*-white in America's odious racial hierarchy. This was especially true for those assigned to the bottom rung. Because those who are classified as Black are the quintessential embodiment of all that is not white, they are likely to suffer the most from this sociopolitical arrangement. Because those who are white perceive themselves as superior to all other races, there are two major advantages that they claim for themselves: (1) Because they occupy the top rung of the racial hierarchical ladder, they are entitled to the lion's share of material resources; and (2) they have a rightful claim to exercise as much sociopolitical power as they see fit.

Struck by the huge response that Yancy's letter generated, and the fact that many respondents were irate about his "Christmas message," I was curious as to what he had actually said in that letter that it provoked such ire. My subsequent reading of his letter determined that the tone of it was respectful, but also firm in his expression of dismay regarding the state of current race relations in the United States. It is important to note that 2015 was near the end of the second term of the first African American president of the United States. (In some minds, Barack Obama's reelection in 2012 should have established with "certainty" that America had indeed entered the post-racial era. However, the realization that the myth of having conquered racism was exposed as the wishful thinking of progressive and liberal whites who were too eager to close the book on this country's allegiance to white supremacy.) Many Black people were not at all surprised by the subsequent backlash against African Americans and their continuous challenge to our country's twofold practices of social exclusion: (1) The sociopolitical hypocrisy that America upholds the cherished ideals of liberty and justice for all; and (2) America's religious hypocrisy of its commitment to the values of a "Judeo-Christian" ethic. After all, the early settlers who came to this British colony were Christians who were seeking relief from religious persecution in England.[1] The idea of a Black two-term president of the United States, talk of the "browning of America," with immigrants from the Global South, American businesses moving overseas, and a growing unrest of conservatives and emerging ultra-right, disaffected whites all made this seem inevitable.

---

1 The Black religious historian Albert J. Raboteau is my source for the concept of "the twofold hypocrisy." See Albert J. Raboteau, *Slave Religion: "The Invisible Institution" in the Antebellum South* (Oxford University Press, 1980). Black abolitionist, David Walker, was the first in a long line of Black writers who indicted America for its double hypocrisy on both sociopolitical and religious grounds. See David Walker, *Walker's Appeal to the Coloured citizens of the world, but in particular, and very expressly, to those of the United States of America*, 3rd and last ed. (1830), introd. James Turner (Black Classic Press, 1993). Others who would note this same twofold double critique would include James Pennington, Henry Highland Garnet, Samuel Ringgold Ward, Frederick Douglass, and Martin Luther King Jr.

Despite the fact that Yancy's letter was not a diatribe from an "angry Black man," but a well-reasoned, measured plea for white Americans to do some soul-searching to determine the degree to which Americans of all racial/ethnic groups could address racial tensions rationally and constructively, the reaction from respondents indicated a resounding "no." I was not surprised that some readers would not welcome what he had to say. However, what was surprising to him (and horrifying for me) was that many of the responders lashed out at him *personally*, with *ad hominem* attacks that were vile, vitriolic, and vulgar, and laced page after page with crude profanity. The reaction was taken seriously enough by university security personnel. They monitored the floor where his campus office was located and university staff were forbidden to give out the location of his office. When on campus, he stayed locked in his office, only meeting with students in his classes who made pre-arranged appointments and were cautiously ushered into his sanctuary. For quite some time he felt unsafe. Truth-telling can be hazardous to one's health.

As a Black woman who has written about, taught classes, and spoken to small and large groups on the topic of race, I was not surprised that there was negative feedback in the comments to Yancy's "Christmas letter" to whites. Yancy also expected to receive *some* unfavorable responses. However, he had not anticipated the virulent, unhinged responses to his missive. (To be fair in characterizing the mail he received, there were also positive, thoughtful comments among the respondents.) The extreme responses of those who commented were not simply "angry," but rather their responses were vitriolic, vile, and vulgar, and laced through and through with profanity. Not only that but there were quite a number of death threats. Before he admitted students to his campus office, he vetted them before he would allow them to enter his space.[2]

George Yancy's experience has not stopped him from continuing his work as a self-described Christian philosopher and author. The responses he received revealed to me that those who chose to respond in an utterly disrespectful way toward him did so because they not only resented that he challenged their cherished ideas and his observations struck them at a deep place in their psyche, but it was also very clear to me that their abusive correspondence was racially motivated. They lobbed vicious epithets that reflected nothing but a deep contempt for the stereotypical "uppity" Black man who would dare to reach out to white readers in an "accusatory" manner. They were unaware that he was a productive human being, a highly educated scholar whose teaching and writing presumably have made a difference in the lives of his students and general readers of his work. What is more, the respondents were uninterested in honest discussion. They did not view him as having anything in common with themselves.

---

2 Some wrote whole pages of nothing else but expletives and were dismissive that he was an accomplished academic, because at the end of the day, he was still a "nigger." See George Yancy, *Backlash: What Happens When We Talk Honestly About Racism in America*, foreword by Cornel West (Rowman & Littlefield, 2018), 25–34.

With eyes to see but unable to perceive, they were incapable of or unwilling to view him in his full humanity, with all the rights and privileges that other citizens enjoy without the threat of harassment or violence. It strikes me that when anyone speaks publicly or writes for public consumption on race, they are taking on a potentially dangerous work for the sake of racial justice. It also tells me that in the body politic there is a segment of whites who are mean-spirited, contemptuous of Blacks, and dangerous. This kind of vitriol toward African Americans is not a single, isolated event.

I recount this story of George Yancy because I think it is important that those who engage in the work of racial justice understand and are made aware of the physical risks and emotional trauma of hearing, reading, and observing attitudes and conduct of those who are unable or unwilling to reckon with how a distorted idea is harmful not only to others but oneself. Moreover, the work of advocating for racial justice is psychologically costly and sometimes thankless; yet, it is unimaginable not to do what one can to change minds and hearts. Nevertheless, people of color face resistance from whites to the idea that they may harbor racist ideas, beliefs, and biases of which they may not be fully conscious. Particularly among those who see themselves as "good people," fair-minded, supportive of equality, who might never have dreamt that although outwardly they project good will, even friendliness, toward persons of other races, their resistance speaks volumes to those on the receiving end of gestures of bad faith.

Fighting the ideology of white supremacy is not a personal, individual thing from which we may try to excuse ourselves from any responsibility because, personally, we are "good" people who have learned what is appropriate or not, what is socially acceptable or not. We cannot simply "refrain" from acting, thinking, or believing harmful things and content ourselves and distance ourselves from any responsibility for continuing to challenge others because we ourselves are on the "right side" of the issue.

The "impediments" to racial reconciliation or to cross-racial dialogue with mutuality and respect that follow are not an exhaustive list. Anyone who is hired or volunteers to work in the area of race relations, anti-racism, or diversity training, in which the constituency you are serving is predominately white, may well have read or heard one or more of the comments I have listed below. Robin DiAngelo, author of *White Fragility: Why It's So Hard for White People to Talk About Racism*, has excellent ones on her list, which arose out of the resistance she has encountered as a racial justice trainer.[3] My list arises out of my own experiences in teaching, preaching on occasion, and facilitating occasional workshops, as well as injudicious comments on articles, blogs, and newspaper stories that in some way are related to the topic of race. The latter sources may not be "scientific" or always unimpeachable, but I believe they offer insight as to how the topic of race evokes visceral reactions and resistance to

3 Robin DiAngelo: *White Fragility: Why It's So Hard for White People to Talk About Racism* (Beacon Press, 2018).

changing not only one's views, but, even more importantly, one's willingness to engage in the work of racial justice. In and of themselves, they do not seem menacing or especially racist. However, what they reveal is a lack of familiarity with important aspects of the significance of African Americans in American history, as well as the present challenges we are facing in regard to fatal encounters of Black men, women, and children with police officers.

In the remainder of this chapter, I will identify attitudes and beliefs that indicate psychological and emotional barriers to racial reconciliation. If we are committed to the work of racial justice, we need to be aware of the underlying fears, anger, and stereotypical mindset and heart-set that keep people tied to ways of thinking that support the status quo. Their goal is to strengthen, not weaken, the hold on too many at the top of the racial hierarchy who have placed their "faith," or "ultimate concern" in things that will keep the social-political structures in place. Understanding the underlying perceptions that help keep this ideology secure will allow those working toward racial justice to propose measures that can get at the heart of what keeps white supremacy in place.

Below is a list of statements which reveal attitudes, mental dispositions, and anger from a fear of both the loss of a position of social dominance or the perquisites that can come from being "white," and the principle existential threat of Black antipathy.[4] Black people are perceived as the quintessential expression of all that is not white. I would not argue

4 Black people seem to symbolize the ultimate threat to "whiteness."

that all whites feel that way—at least not consciously. However, I must mention the statement James Baldwin once made regarding the concept of the "negro" in the imagination of those ensnared in "whiteness."

Baldwin stated:

> What white people have to do is try and find out in their own hearts why it was necessary to have a "nigger" in the first place, because I'm not a nigger, I'm a man. But if you think I'm a nigger, it means you *need* him. The question that you've got to ask yourself, the white population of this country has got to ask itself, North and South because it's one country and for a Negro there is no difference between the North and the South—it's just a difference in the way they castrate you, but the fact of the castration is the American fact.... If I'm not the nigger here and you invented him, you the white people invented him, then you've got to find out why. And the future of the country depends on that, whether or not it is able to ask that question.[5]

Baldwin's assertion regarding the term "nigger," which in current public discourse we have euphemized, as though we adults are not grown up enough to address the underlying

---

5 In this quote of a statement that James Baldwin made in 1962, he actually used the term "nigger," which whites often hurled at Black people as a term of utter disrespect. I have chosen not to substitute the more palatable term "negro" for the word "nigger," to evoke the contempt and disdain with which white people felt free to express to Black people. Baldwin's comment is taken from the 2016 documentary about James Baldwin titled *I Am Not Your Negro*, dir. Raoul Peck (Magnolia Home Entertainment Studio, 2016), DVD.

embarrassment and shame of racial intolerance rather than face the discomfort of knowing that racism is built upon the irrational distortion of "whiteness" thinking. Insistence upon candor about why it would be necessary to invent the word "nigger," in the first place, should be a first step of liberation from those who espouse white superiority. The philosopher George Yancy has a thought-provoking discussion of the epithet "nigger," which examines further how foul this epithet is when employed across racial lines.[6]

Below each statement, I will comment on what message those statements convey to me as a Black woman who is committed to the work of racial justice.

WILLFUL IGNORANCE OF OR INDIFFERENCE TO AMERICAN HISTORY

There is a persistent denial that race relations is a real problem. White people like to remind us that things are certainly better than they were in the days of Jim Crow. Not having had to endure the dehumanization of Jim Crow themselves, white people seem to view themselves as capable of assessing the degree of "progress" that has been made as a result of the Civil Rights Movement. In discussions of enslavement and segregation we are told that these historical situations were not necessarily as bad as some Black people say they were. Moreover, politically conservative whites reject

6 See Yancy, *Backlash*, 1–54.

any notion of systemic or structural racism. Liberal whites believe, in theory, that Blacks got a raw deal; but interestingly, too many are not committed to renouncing their privilege to self-identify as white—and all that comes with it, as the legacy of whiteness lives on.

Denial of racism and lamenting racism but wanting to be our "allies" are impotent positions to take in assessing the feasibility of dismantling white supremacy. The resistance to the idea of white supremacy and commiserating about it, yet continuing to support it by inaction against it and collusion with it, ensures that the result will remain the same. Any notion of "reform" is only nibbling around the edges—it is not enough to *dismantle* a structure from which they ultimately benefit. Either way, Black communities continue on, struggle through, reconciled to the possibility that, if change does come, it will transform their lives in the here and now. The outcome, by and large, remains the same. Thus, we inch along in the struggle like glowworms.

Sociologists David Embrick, J. Scott Carter, and Cameron Lippard observe that a "majority" of whites are "satisfied" with the way Blacks have been treated. These whites assert that Blacks are being treated fairly at work, in restaurants, stores, neighborhoods, theaters, and bars, and getting treatment from physicians.[7] The authors speak of a *lack of empathy* on the part of whites to *our* experiences under the

7 David G. Embrick, J. Scott Carter, and Cameron D. Lippard, "Introduction," in *Protecting Whiteness: Whitelash and the Rejection of Racial Equality* (University of Washington Press, 2020), 3–23.

thumb of white dominance. There are whites who wish to maintain that race is no longer the issue that it once was. If Black people are *not* doing as well as others, it is because of either failings on our part, limits to our intelligence, our low morals, laziness because we lack a work ethic, or because we make bad choices, especially in the accused propensity of Black women to have babies out of wedlock in hopes of collecting "government handouts" while refusing to work.

DEI (DIVERSITY, EQUITY, INCLUSION) HIRES

"America has always been a meritocracy."

"We need to go back to hiring, promoting, and enrolling in higher education the 'best qualified' candidates."

DEI is treated as the latest "scheme" for hiring or promoting minoritized "unqualified" candidates at the expense of "highly qualified" white males. Opponents of DEI believe with great certainty that diversity candidates (persons of color) are, by definition, "unqualified," and have only been selected because the institution in question wants to give the *appearance* of commitment to "diversity." If a candidate of color is actually selected, critics of DEI automatically assume that the candidate is either "unqualified" and/or "totally incompetent." If the unselected candidate is white, then that candidate was the "most qualified" and yet another "highly qualified candidate" is passed over in favor of an "undeserving DEI candidate." This hiring process will have taken away opportunities from deserving/qualified (white males). This, white critics maintain, is "reverse discrimination."

Black people are said to be *un*willing to abide by the established "rules" that this country runs on "meritocracy," that if you "work hard, do the right thing," and adopt "American values," then you will "succeed." Black people are unwilling to follow or incapable of following the rules and mores of "normal" people. (White people are the "norm.") Vocal whites cannot embrace the goal of "equity," because "equity" means (to them) that "everyone gets the same thing." Given the resistance to DEI, it is clear that a sizeable percentage of white people, consciously or subconsciously, do not perceive Black people as deserving being viewed as "equal" to them nor should there be an acknowledgment and correction of existing biases and historical inequality. (This refusal betrays a lack of any sincere intention to make amends for the sake of racial justice.)

REVERSE DISCRIMINATION

Whites, especially males, are beginning to complain that they are being discriminated against (suffering "reverse discrimination") because they are being denied jobs or admission to colleges or graduate schools due to policies that "give" these opportunities to Black people, other minorities, and women. White males perceive themselves as being frozen out of opportunities for advancement. By definition, anyone not white and/or not male and heterosexual is "*un*qualified" for advancement. "They are taking jobs from white males." The underlying assumption is that non-whites are all assumed now to be DEI candidates. This ignores the reality that white males are still *overwhelmingly* represented in corporate America and many other leadership opportunities. There is a disparity between what whites *perceive* and what the reality is. By casting aspersions on programs geared toward breaking both the homogeneity and hegemony of race/ethnicity, gender, and other protected classes, critics undermine efforts to open up opportunities for qualified minorities and women to compete for admission to college and university programs, and hiring and promotion job opportunities.

ZERO-SUM GAME

Our efforts toward equality are viewed as being done at the expense of whites. Equality of Blacks places whites at a "disadvantage." Affirmative action put "unqualified Blacks" in places that they did not earn at the expense of "highly qualified" whites. In challenging affirmative action, and now, dismantling DEI, we are retreating from diversity, equity, and inclusion. I have yet to find serious efforts to substitute these measures with mechanisms that do not also harm whites, in order to rectify previous harm done to Black people. However, I see attitudes such as this as a confirmation that not everyone embraces equality. There *is* no interest in rectifying anything. Those classified as "white" believe that they have been and are *entitled* to as many opportunities to advance as possible. Those classified as "Black" have never been "entitled" to anything. The pretense of affirming equality is just that, "pretense." The real "favored" group (white males) is not interested in "equality." There is a repudiation of equality because it interferes with the perks of occupying the top rung of the racial hierarchy. The ongoing struggle rests with the commitment to live and love our way through resistance to achieving racial justice. The challenge for those who wish to commit to the struggle for racial justice is to learn how to participate in it or not to retreat from the commitment to level the playing field, but also to educate disaffected whites to understand "privilege" in the context of racism. Privilege, in this context, is not about economic prosperity. It is really about the advantages that being classified as "white" brings. More favorable assumptions are granted to whites because they are more readily assumed to *belong* in a given social setting, such as a position of authority or leadership in an institution. Black people and other persons of color are much less often perceived as having authority. A Black man can still be assumed to be a janitor, not an attorney, banker, or supervisor. A Black woman can still be mistaken for a cafeteria worker or a worker in housekeeping. Latinx/ Hispanic women might be seen as the one who dusts and empties trash cans in an office building, not necessarily an executive. In a room of white professionals except for one Black woman, the question on everyone else's mind is: "Does *she* belong in this group?" In such scenarios, whites are far less likely to have their presence questioned, even silently.

"Raising the issue of race is 'racist' and 'divisive,' and enables the perpetual victimhood of minorities."

Talking about race is now considered "divisive." The plea of some whites is to focus on what "unites" us. Meanwhile, race is never to be discussed. Raising the topic of race is viewed to be rude and accusatory. This message is a manipulative tactic to silence the voices of those who may perceive that a statement or action is racist. Such persons who raise the topic of race may be rebuked and told that things are "all right now." Things are much improved from what they were. In other words, Blacks have nothing to complain about now. It seems as though there is a sense that the sociopolitical gains of the Civil Rights Movement were enough to have brought full racial justice.

To say that something is "racist," or to call a white person a racist, is now judged to be in itself racist. This is a tactic to deflect by turning the tables on the person of color. It is certainly a "conversation stopper!" Persons of color are left with this message: "Racism without racists."[8]

8 This is a major theme in Eduardo Bonilla-Silva's book, *Racism without Racists: Color-Blind Racism and the Persistence of Racial Inequality in the United States*, 6th ed. (Rowman & Littlefield, 2021).

EMPATHETIC IMAGINATION

More than once, I have known someone to raise the question of how it is that many other immigrants have come to this country and have managed to be assimilated into this society over time. Why haven't African Americans, who've been here for centuries been able to do this? The suggestion is that the experiences of Europeans who immigrated to the United States were analogous to the experiences of those who were brought to the United States for enslavement. Anyone who has any familiarity with the experiences of those who were brought here from Africa in chains during the Atlantic slave trade knows that the journey from West Africa to North America was one that lasted on average approximately eighty days, under conditions unfit for animals. For those captured for enslavement, the journey was a pure nightmare for those who survived it. Some of the Africans captured in Africa and loaded on ships opted for suicide in the open sea rather than complete the journey.[9]

Although some European immigrants were not treated well initially, eventually they could assimilate. Black people were stigmatized and had conferred upon them a pariah status to ensure that they would not be permitted to live among white people as social equals, *ever.* The false equivalency between European immigrants and enslaved Black people reveals the profound ignorance of the speaker. Enslaved

---

9 See George Francis Dow, *Slave Ships and Slaving* (General Publishing Company, 2002); Marcus Rediker, *The Slave Ship: A Human History* (Penguin, 2008).

Blacks were *never* intended to "assimilate" in American society as social equals.

I fully acknowledge that, for some immigrant Europeans, it was initially difficult to be accepted in the United States. They were victims of ghettoizing, viewed as carriers of disease, and they were viewed as not "white" enough, but as white "ethnics." However, within a relatively short period of time they were treated as productive middle-class people, to the extent that they were willing to abandon the languages and cultural practices which had shaped their lives prior to immigration. Unsurprisingly, African Americans, with typical physical features of many of African descent, could never "assimilate." The particularized features that readily point to our "otherness," such as hair texture, skin color, nose shape, lip size, and bodily physique, are the very "identifiers" that caught the attention of white colonizers in the first place. Moreover, pseudo-scientific racism adherents tried to link the physiological features to attempt to justify the subjugation of African Americans, in perpetuity.

"My family did not own slaves. We had no part in what happened in the past."

The underlying point in such assertions is that contemporary whites have no responsibility for what happened in the past. Therefore, it would be unjust to "punish" white people for the sins of their fathers. What is troubling is that there is no acknowledgment that they have been unfairly advantaged by the "whiteness" of their foreparents, which continues to grant them privileges. Those that are white continue *as a collective* to retain the immoral benefits of their ancestors, in the current system. Dissociating themselves from any responsibility of continuing in the ideology of white supremacy now, denying complicity, enjoying the fruits of white supremacy, and not taking a role in challenging that supremacy, as they have continued to enjoy and claim the advantages of whiteness, sounds like a recipe for maintaining the status quo, *indefinitely*. Some white people would prefer to minimize what had transpired in the past and continue enjoying the fruits of their status. They see no reason to alter what took place in the past. They decline to play any role in dismantling an unjust social order. The implication is that they cannot be blamed or held accountable for a system they did not set up. They may have had some "advantages," but they have worked hard for everything they have. There are no recourses for non-whites. There is no redress. Today's whites are innocent. Where is there a space for considering making amends? Besides, most whites are not rich; there are whites who have struggled and continue to struggle economically. They do not believe that they benefit from being classified white. What they fail to understand is that, superficially, they can or do have the "advantage" of not being Black. Secretly, or perhaps not so secretly, they aspire to access the same advantages as whites with a higher income than they could earn.

"You people are always bringing up slavery. Can't you just get past it?" *"Why can't Black people just get past it?"*

Comments of this kind highlight a total dismissal of the lived experiences of Black people. Such comments are intended to keep Black people silent. Many of us would *love* to "get past it." The "it" that Black people cannot seem to leave in the past is that the past is still very much present. Opportunities to acquire property and land were denied to many of our parents and foreparents. The Homestead Act left Black people out. Access to housing intended to increase the size of the middle class was denied to Black people explicitly, by the federal government, in collusion with the home construction industry, banking institutions, and real estate companies, which knew that white homeowners believed that neighborhoods in which Black people had housing would necessarily experience drops in real estate value. Restrictive covenants kept Blacks from buying homes in white neighborhoods, further limiting opportunities to buy homes, and Black World War II veterans were purposely denied access to the benefits of the GI Bill.[10]

Eminent domain was used as a way of destroying housing in Black neighborhoods, leaving the segregated residents homeless. Builders refused to make available houses for Black

10 My maternal grandfather and his youngest brother participated in the Normandy invasion, June 6, 1944. A third brother participated in the battle of Anzio, Italy, January 22 to June 4, 1944. Despite their honorable service and the risk of loss of life and limb, upon their return to the United States, they were once again "Negroes."

buyers, restricting Black people's access to white neighborhoods because whites were insistent that they be free of the presence of Black people, to uphold segregation. Literally, walls were built to separate white people from Black people. When public housing projects were built, white people had ready access to them first, and housing for whites would be vacant while there was a large waiting for list for Blacks who needed public housing.

So, no, we cannot just "get past it."

AN INVITATION

The purpose of this chapter was to lay out some of the ways in which those of us engaged in the work of racial justice, or those who would like to commit to the struggle, can get exposure to the challenges of participating in the struggle rather than complaining about it. These gatherings are a way of getting a sense of what people think or attitudes they hold in the context of race. They are also an opportunity to think about how to enter into the arena for the sake of being transformed by cross-racial engagement; and perhaps, accompanying others who join in this work.

This book in its entirety is an invitation to whites to consider the extent to which they may be called upon to join all those who are concerned with how one may prepare oneself for stepping into the breach. There is plenty of room for all of us to take our place in this struggle. All who are interested must step into the breach. I have noted some of the challenges that one may meet in hopes that, in one way or another, one will be called upon to get involved, and in so doing one may contribute in some way to help "make this world a little better than you found it".[11]

---

11 This saying has been attributed to Robert Baden-Powell.

CHAPTER 5

Toward Racial Healing

I have been engaged in the study of human rights and human dignity for more than a quarter of a century. In various ways I have taken up the challenge of engaging in the struggle for racial justice. I have sometimes felt frustration when engaging well-intended participants in challenging white supremacy seminars at which there are some—again, well-intended—participants who want to rush immediately to reconciliation. Reconciliation is a process, not an event. The goal of reconciliation requires a commitment to do the work required to become skillful in interfacing with others across racial lines. It is in the course of such encounters that we come to know more about who we are, and what our interpersonal strengths and weaknesses are. We also prepare ourselves for skillful engagement in personal self-examination to determine what influences have shaped us in racial interrelations (and other barriers of distance), with the goal of developing practices that facilitate constructive engagement with others who are "different" from ourselves. Not only would a spiritual practice of one's choice that helps one address interior and exterior issues when engaging in small groups and larger community settings be fruitful in work related to white supremacy, but I also believe such a practice helps when one is preparing for the hard work involved in emotionally charged discussions on race. Attention to such work can contribute to a general sense of well-being and lessen the tensions that can arise from difficult conversations.

What would be needed to move into a position where we can speak meaningfully about what racial reconciliation would look like in our context? I maintain that we cannot simply gather in groups and start talking about "dismantling" white supremacy, as if we know what that is. We *can* talk meaningfully about racial reconciliation—at some point. But first, we need a clear diagnosis of that which interferes with our capacity to recognize ourselves in one another.

THE CHALLENGE OF REPAIRING MISTAKES OF THE PAST

How does a society make amends for correcting historical wrongs? Disaffected blue-collar whites have long resented the idea of minorities being "given opportunities," for they perceive that our gain always means their loss. The only thing that they could see was that whites may have been "robbed" of opportunities that were denied to them, and that those who were granted these opportunities were "unqualified" and "undeserving." The position of some whites has been that one does not correct a wrong by performing another wrong, for two wrongs do not make a right. There is a logic to the critique of such programs, although the critique of these initiatives was intended to address discrimination that was practiced toward persons of color and white women as well. I strongly suspect that those who criticize the current remedies are not particularly concerned about remedying historical "wrongs," so no ideas or suggestions are ever offered to address discrimination of the past; moreover, their concern is for protecting the continued advantageous access of white males rather than righting past wrongs. Some whites are unwilling to concede that there really was discrimination at all, for they would rather believe that minorities already have equal opportunity to compete. If they worked hard and applied themselves, they could get ahead. Others are quick to denigrate anyone selected as an affirmative action hire or a diversity, equity, inclusion (DEI) hire as by definition *un*qualified, believing that *only* a (white) male candidate is "naturally" the best qualified. The fact that these assertions are unsubstantiated but treated as fact betrays bias, if not flat-out racism, reveals a keen sense of entitlement, and demonstrates neither open-mindedness nor the capacity or desire for being fair-minded.

My point is that I strongly sense that there is no desire to remedy opportunities denied to minoritized students. What critics really want is for minorities to overlook what has been done, rightly or wrongly, and accept the assigned status to which we were born. It does not seem to matter that the failure to rectify harm from past discriminatory practices ensures that discrimination persists and leaves a segment of the population perpetually disadvantaged.

We live in a season of racial resentment. You can see it quite openly in public discourse. We can see it in the acting out of some members of the radical right-wing of the Republican Party and in groups who are talking about "white power." There are some white conservative voices who feel that Black people are now the "favored" racial group. They view themselves as being victims of "reverse discrimination." They maintain that they are being locked out of opportunities because they are neither a white female nor a racial minority. Along with that, there has been a campaign against DEI that has been even more vilified than affirmative action once was. Critics of affirmative action have viewed the program as "taking white jobs," even though it has been said that the group most helped by affirmative action was white women. With DEI, as with affirmative action, any candidate who is hired or promoted as a result of DEI consideration by definition is automatically perceived as "unqualified," apart from being viewed as fitting one of the desirable categories for "special" consideration. It would seem that the best qualified candidate for any job is now a white male and that white males are entitled to jobs and promotions because they are white males.

I raise this issue because it makes me wonder to what extent whites really desire racial reconciliation. I know that there are white people who long for justice and peace as much as I do; and they back up that desire with committed activism But I think it is important to have a conversation regarding how much opposition or resistance will come from those who are neither ready for nor interested in an improvement in race relations.

The sense is that a core group of whites prefers things to remain as they are—with historical wrongs unremedied. There is also a sense of white male entitlement that is blind to the facts and a huge lack of empathetic imagination. They presume that they are *always* better qualified than anyone else. By definition, Blacks and other minorities are perceived as "less qualified" or never more qualified than white candidates. They believe that only "the most qualified" should ever be hired, admitted, or promoted: the principle of meritocracy. "That's the way it has *always* been done." In those responses there is no sense of the systematic historical denial of opportunities for Black people or other minorities to advance. There have been no remedies to address the past and it seems that this is as it should be. Otherwise, the advance of other races denies whites unfettered opportunities to get what they want or to what they are (always) entitled. The disturbing feeling is that we are indeed operating from a zero-sum mindset. If this is really true, I see no real prospect of rectifying past wrongs.

They feel safe with their cherished myth that the United States has always been based upon merit. Having had long experience in hiring and promoting candidates (in my earlier life!), I'm clearly aware of the presence of the reality of the "old boy network," hiring based upon knowing someone who knows someone.

This concern is sharpened by attitudes that are often voiced in public discourse. Whites feel that Black people have already received "all opportunities to catch up." The playing field is level. (There is no basis upon which they make this assertion.) If Blacks do not succeed, it is on them. They have not "tried hard enough" or "worked hard enough" or they do not have the aptitude to succeed. We are told that Black people want things handed to them; that they do not want to "earn" anything that they get. They always have their hands out. If Black males did not have criminal propensities and worked for a living, then they could advance. And if Black women would not have children out of wedlock, then the Black community could flourish. Yet, at the same time, we are "reminded" that Black people, by nature, are unintelligent, not disciplined, not equipped to succeed in (white) society. Either way, the plight of Black people lies within them. Thus, white consciences are free. The trafficking in negative stereotypes and false narratives leads me to question to what extent a majority of whites are committed to the notion of a change in the way we interface across racial lines.

NO RECONCILIATION WITHOUT A DAY OF RECKONING

There can be no genuine reconciliation without a day of reckoning. I contend that before we can begin to speak seriously about reconciliation there are at least eight things that would need to happen. First, we would need to be courageous enough to tell the truth about United States history. Second, as citizens of this country, we would have to come to grips with the very flawed nature of our Founding Fathers, and see them in all of their human complexities and contradictions. Third, we would have to deal with the flawed nature of our nation's founding documents, which never resolved the discrepancy of constitutional support for an economic system of perpetual servitude while extolling the virtues of liberty and freedom. Fourth, we would have to abandon the myth of American exceptionalism. Fifth, we would have to make critical adjustments to our economic system to address economic inequality. Sixth, we would have to alter patterns of interaction and engagement in the economic, social, cultural, and political realms. Seventh, we would have to acknowledge our long-standing political and religious hypocrisy regarding the treatment of African Americans and other minority groups. Finally, reparation is warranted to *repair* the harm of enslavement that robbed Black people of their labor for generations to come. Right now, we cannot even have a conversation about what reparations would look like or how they could be accomplished without massive displacement.

"Repair" is what reparations are about. It is repair of what was denied, broken, misguided, and evil. Along with thinking through this repair, we have to consider how to move toward that new beginning which I have mentioned. Only then will we have the conditions for the possibility of genuine racial reconciliation.

WITHOUT METANOIA, HEALING AND RECONCILIATION ARE IMPOSSIBLE

Whatever is needed for *genuine reconciliation*, whether between husbands and wives, two groups within a local church, two or more races in American society, or two nations in the global community, I think the ingredients are the same. We need a commitment to genuine metanoia; that is, a soul-penetrating repentance, a willingness to forgive, and a longing for the kind of justice that makes for true peace. When there is a breach in a relationship there must be an airing of our differences, an unshakeable commitment to metanoia, and the willingness of the aggrieved party to forgive, if there is any hope for reconciliation. On the one hand, the offender must turn aside from the offending action with a commitment to avoid the risk of ever offending again.

On the other hand, the offended must surrender the impulse to embrace perpetual victimhood. Of course, dealing with both inclinations is likely to be easier said than done! This is particularly true of forgiveness. Anyone who has ever been wronged or treated unjustly and disrespectfully knows how difficult it can be to forgive. To counsel forgiveness in the face of injustice feels like pouring salt on a searing burn. To suggest to the victimized that they must practice "forgiveness" in the context of injustice can seem heartless, as if one is oblivious or indifferent to the pain that injustice brings.

However, what happens to us when we *refuse* to forgive? The taste of *un*forgiveness is bitter. The rage that injustice evokes can erode the soul like cancer. When we refuse to forgive, unforgiveness exacts a cost from us. To forgive is neither surrendering to defacement nor is it accepting maltreatment. Forgiveness is the refusal to be consumed with hatred toward the abuser or submission to ill-will. It is restraining from retaliation and a desire for revenge. This is why racial justice work requires intentional, consistent practices that strengthen one's spiritual resources. One may opt not to profess a particular religious tradition. It may well help, but it is not required to work for justice. It is essential, however, that one is attentive to tending one's inner resources to preclude bringing one's maladaptive coping with anger, adversity, ill-will, bitterness, and so on into the arena of justice-making work. Early on, those who participated on the frontlines of civil rights activism viewed attention to one's internal life as *essential* to withstand the resistance, anger, resentful of those in the Civil Rights Movement.[1]

---

1 See writings of the following spiritual leaders and/or civil rights activists: Howard Thurman, John Lewis, James Lawson, Bayard Rustin, and Pauli Murray.

JUSTICE

The journey to reconciliation requires repentance and forgiveness, but it also requires justice. Each side must be willing to forego selfish interests for the sake of forging a peace that can support all. Victims must forego their impulse for revenge and perpetrators of injustice must forego their desire to escape accountability. The oppressed must be given the space to lament the deep wounds that seep down from generation to generation. But they also must surrender the right to retribution or retaliation. Oppressors have to have the courage to face their guilt and shame. The oppressor must also resist the temptation to want to casually let "bygones be bygones" in the temptation to pretend that they have not benefited and do not continue to benefit from the privileged status of being white in a society governed not by siblinghood, but by the notion that white people are innately superior. In the United States, where there remains the undercurrent of distrust and resentment between the races, would that people would clamor for a venue in which the unfortunate legacy of slavery and the system of Jim Crow and its remnants could be addressed honestly, humbly, and constructively, so that we and our ancestors on both sides could truly rest in peace. Peace between the races will be impossible if there is little or no attempt to make amends for the past, along with a heartfelt commitment to justice-making in our economic, social, political, and cultural life together, now and in the future.

PEACE

Finally, the journey to reconciliation requires not only repentance, forgiveness, and justice, but also a commitment to peace. Peace is not the absence of conflict or war. It is a *byproduct* of justice-making and is something that must be worked on by *all* parties involved. We seem to take for granted that *everyone* wants peace. As a student of human nature in the context of history and current affairs, I am not certain about that at all. My sense is that people may well desire peace for *themselves*, but not necessarily for others. For a contemporary example, as I think about the intransigence that affects both sides of the Israeli–Palestinian conflict, I would surmise that what is missing in the search for peace is a desire for the welfare of the Other that is as fierce as the desire for one's own. Globally, we live in a state of organized "non-peace." Without justice, there will be no real peace at all.

A theological critique of how we humans behave recognizes that, however enlightened we believe we are, we are limited in our knowledge and understanding not only of God but also ourselves. We do not know or understand all that there is to know about the human body, soul, and mind. Our experiences should lead us to recognize that we may well be ill-equipped to solve some of the issues that arise out of our capacity to violate the law of love at every turn. The problem of white supremacy, which is incredibly intransigent, will not be resolved by legislation. For example, the laws passed during the Civil Rights Movement did not alter behaviors or attitudes or emotions, and certainly did not address our emotional reactions as to how we engage people who look differently from us. White supremacy is a *heart* issue. We have "been there and done that," circumvented and subverted that which a law of justice might demand.

Meetings and gatherings, denominational statements, speeches and sermons, and adult education classes in and of themselves will not magically lead to a change of heart that reflects metanoia. The problem of race is a theological problem at its core. It has economic, social, political, and cultural dimensions to it. But its *source* is a reflection and embodiment of a disorder in our beliefs; the emotions of fear, greed, hatred, and ignorance, which are indicative of a *heart* problem, lodged in the human will. The ideology of white supremacy is not something we can think our way through. (If we creatures could be really persuaded by "logic" or "sound reasoning," we would have abandoned white supremacy a long time ago.)

A WORD TO THE US CHURCHES

It is one thing to admit the reality of racism within the economic, social, cultural, and political dimensions of life in the United States. It is another thing to have to acknowledge the lingering persistence of racism *within this country's churches* and their failure to take a decisive leadership role in addressing the persistence of racism both inside and outside the churches. Gratefully, a vital segment of our churches has been at the forefront of advocating for the rights of the marginalized, including victims of racial/ethnic discrimination. The efforts of this segment of the churches are to be applauded. However, anti-racist activism is not to be left to self-identified "liberal" or "progressive" segments of the churches. Anti-racist activism should be a task of *anyone* who professes faith in Jesus Christ. I believe that the failure to recognize this as a legitimate task of Christ's disciples is primarily due to the fact that racial/ethnic discrimination is not always understood as a *theological, spiritual* problem at its core.

Unfortunately, too many of our churches have continued to align themselves with those who are either diametrically opposed to supporting the rights of minorities, or those who will either wittingly or unwittingly maintain the status quo out of a misguided belief that discrimination is a "social" problem that has little to do with the "real" mission of the churches, which is to "save souls" and "grow" churches. This failure to understand racism in all its guises as a deeply spiritual pathology allows us to maintain the delusion that we can practice racism *and* worship God "in Spirit and in Truth" at the same time, without harm to our ongoing relationship with God. As long as this mistaken belief persists, our churches will continue to lag *behind* progressive individuals and groups outside the churches, rather than to *lead the way* toward facilitating the practices of true justice and genuine peace.

Bibliography

Bailey, Zinzi. "What Is Structural Racism?" Health Equity. Accessed February 27, 2025. https://www.ama-assn.org/delivering-care/health-equity/what-structural-racism.

Baldwin, James. "On Being White ... and Other Lies." In *The Cross of Redemption, Uncollected Writings*, edited and with an introduction by Randall Kenan. Vintage, 2010.

Barth, Karl. "The First Commandment as an Axiom of Theology." In H. Martin Rumscheidt, *The Way of Theology in Karl Barth, Essays and Comments*, with an introduction by Stephen W. Sykes. Pickwick Publications, 1986.

"Beginnings, Exploration and Colonization." Library of Congress. Accessed February 27, 2025. https://tinyurl.com/46v5td7d.

Bell, Derrick. *Faces at the Bottom of the Well*. Rev. ed. Basic Books, 2018.

Bird, Kevin A., John P. Jackson Jr., and Andrew Winston. "Confronting Scientific Racism in Psychology: Lessons from Evolutionary Biology and Genetics." *American Psychologist* 79, no. 4 (2024), 497–508. https://doi.org/10.1037/amp0001228.

Bonilla-Silva, Eduardo. *Racism without Racists: Color-Blind Racism and the Persistence of Racial Inequality in the United States*. 6th ed. Rowman & Littlefield, 2021.

Brown, Matt. "Trump's Debate References to 'Black Jobs' and 'Hispanic Jobs' Stir Democratic Anger." *Associated Press*, June 28, 2024.

Calvin, John. *Institutes of the Christian Religion*. Book I, XI. The Westminster Press, 1970.

Coates, Ta-Nehisi. *Between the World and Me*. Spiegel & Grau, 2015.

Cole, Nicki Lisa. "Theories of Ideology: The Concept and Its Relationship to Marxist Theory." ThoughtCo, July 3, 2019. https://www.thoughtco.com/ideology-definition-3026356.

Cooke, Sam. "A Change Is Gonna Come." RCA Victor, 1964.

Dabashi, Hamid. "White Is Not a Colour—White Is an Ideology." Al Jazeera, July 23, 2021. https://www.aljazeera.com/opinions/2021/7/23/white-is-not-a-colour-white-is-an-ideology.

Dawsey, Josh. "From Conspiracy Theories to 'Shithole' Countries: Trump's Thoroughly Absurd Thursday." *The Washington Post*, January 12, 2018.

Des Pres, Terrence. *The Survivor: An Anatomy of Life in the Death Camps*. Oxford University Press, 1976.

DiAngelo, Robin. *White Fragility: Why It's So Hard for White People to Talk About Racism*. Foreword by Michael Eric Dyson. Beacon Press, 2018.

Dow, George Francis. *Slave Ships and Slaving*. General Publishing Company, 2002.

Dubois, W. E. B. *The Souls of Black Folks*. A. C. McClurg, 1903.

Eagleton, Terry. *Ideology: An Introduction*. Verso, 1991.

Eckstein, Yechiel. "Jewish Concepts: Judaism on the Worth of Every Person." Jewish Virtual Library. Accessed February 20, 2025. https://www.jewishvirtuallibrary.org/judaism-on-the-worth-of-every-person.

Embrick, David G., J. Scott Carter, and Cameron D. Lippard. "Introduction." In *Protecting Whiteness: Whitelash and the Rejection of Racial Equality*. University of Washington Press, 2020.

Gaita, Raimond. *A Common Humanity: Thinking About Love and Truth and Justice*. Routledge, 2000.

Gray, Bradley. "The Gods We Make vs. the God We Need." 1517: Christ for You, January 25, 2022. https://tinyurl.com/5n8t3mwn.

"Historical Foundations of Race." National Museum of African American History and Culture (NMAACH). Accessed February 27, 2025. https://nmaahc.si.edu/learn/talking-about-race/topics/historical-foundations-race.

Hoover, Heidi. "Treat Every Person with Dignity." My Jewish Learning, August 26, 2014. https://www.myjewishlearning.com/rabbis-without-borders/treat-every-person-with-dignity.

"The Immigration Act of 1924 (The Johnson-Reed Act)." Office of the Historian. Accessed February 27, 2025. https://history.state.gov/milestones/1921-1936/immigration-act.

"The Indians at the Time of Contact, 1600–1850." Library of Congress. Accessed February 27, 2025. https://tinyurl.com/muymc.

"The Islamic Concept of Human Dignity." Akhuwat. Accessed February 20, 2025. https://akhuwatuk.org/the-islamic-concept-of-dignity.

Jenson, Matt. *The Gravity of Sin, Augustine, Luther and Barth on homo incurvatus in se*. T&T Clark, 2006.

Kamali, Mohammad Hashim. "Human Dignity in Islam and Its Impact on Society." *New Straits Times*, October 25, 2017. https://www.nst.

com.my/opinion/columnists/2017/10/294803/human-dignity-islam-and-its-impact-society.

Kelsey, George D. *Racism and the Christian Understanding of Man*. Wipf & Stock, 2001.

Kirkland, Justin. "Toni Morrison Broke Down the Truth About White Supremacy in a Powerful 1993 PBS Interview." *Esquire*, August 6, 2019. https://www.esquire.com/entertainment/books/a28621535/toni-morrison-white-supremacy-charlie-rose-interview-racism.

Levinas, Emmanuel. *Entre Nous: On Thinking-of-the-Other*. Translated by Michael B. Smith and Barbara Harshav. Columbia University Press, 1998.

Lippard, Cameron D., J. Scott Carter, and David G. Embrick. *Protecting Whiteness: Whitelash and the Rejection of Racial Equality*. Foreword by Eduardo Bonilla-Silva. University of Washington Press, 2020.

Lipsitz, George. *The Possessive Investment in Whiteness: How White People Profit from Identity Politics*. Revised and expanded ed. Temple University Press, 2006.

Lodhi, Areesha. "Why Does the US Have Such a High Maternal-Mortality Rate?" Al Jazeera, August 17, 2024.

Luther, Martin. "The First Commandment." In *The Large Catechism of Martin Luther*, edited by Henry Eyster Jacobs. The Lutheran Library Publishing Ministry, 2018.

McVeigh, Myron. "Paul Tillich: Dynamics of Faith." Accessed February 27, 2025. https://www.ukessays.com/essays/religion/paul-tillich-dynamics-faith-summary-7239.php.

Migliore, Daniel J. *Faith Seeking Understanding: An Introduction to Christian Theology*. 2nd ed. Wm B. Eerdmans, 2004.

Miller, Chloe. "'There Is No White Community': Cultural Appropriation and Pop-Culture in the US." University of Notre Dame, September 4, 2023. https://sites.nd.edu/jamesbaldwin/tag/on-being-white.

Mitchell, Beverly Eileen. "The African American Struggle for Human Dignity in Chattel Slavery and Afterwards." In *The Handbook of African American Theology*, edited by Frederick Ware, Antonia Michelle Daymond, and Eric Lewis Williams. T&T Clark, 2019.

Mitchell, Beverly Eileen. *Black Abolitionism: A Quest for Human Dignity*. Orbis Books, 2005.

Mitchell, Beverly Eileen. *Plantations and Death Camps: Religion, Ideology, and Human Dignity*. Fortress Press, 2009.

Moltmann, Jürgen. *God in Creation: A New Theology of Creation and the Spirit of God*. 2nd ed. Fortress Press, 1993.

Morrison, Toni, and Charlie Rose. Partial transcription of an interview. May 7, 1993. https://charlierose.com/videos/18778.

National Association for the Advancement of Colored People (NAACP). "Criminal Fact Sheet." Accessed February 27, 2025. https://tinyurl.com/3v94ebyn.

Niebuhr, Reinhold. *The Nature and Destiny of Man*, vol. 1. Scribner's Sons, 1964.

Oliver, Michael. "James Baldwin and the 'Lie of Whiteness': Toward an Ethic of Culpability, Complicity, and Confession." *Religions* 12, no. 6 (2021), 447. https://doi.org/10.3390/rel12060447.

Peck, Raoul, dir. *I Am Not Your Negro.* Magnolia Home Entertainment Studio, 2017. DVD.

"Permanent Indian Frontier." National Park Service. Accessed February 27, 2025. https://www.nps.gov/articles/pifront.htm.

Raboteau, Albert J. *Slave Religion: "The Invisible Institution" in the Antebellum South.* Oxford University Press, 1980.

Rediker, Marcus. *The Slave Ship: A Human History.* Reprint ed. Penguin, 2008.

Southern Poverty Law Center. "KKK." Accessed March 3, 2025. https://www.splcenter.org/resources/extremist-files/ku-klux-klan.

Thurman, Howard. *The Luminous Darkness.* Reprint. Harper & Row, 1965.

Tillich, Paul. *Dynamics of Faith.* Harper & Row, 2001.

Walker, David. *Walker's Appeal to the Coloured citizens of the world, but in particular, and very expressly, to those of the United States of America, with additional notes, corrections, &c., third and last edition.* Boston, 1830. Reprint, with introduction by James Turner. Black Classic Press, 1993.

Ward, Samuel Ringgold. *Autobiography of a Fugitive Negro: His Anti-Slavery Labours in the United States.* Wipf & Stock, 2000. Originally published in 1855 by John Snow.

Weil, Simone. "What Is Sacred in Every Human Being?" In *Simone Weil: Late Philosophical Writings*, translated by Eric O. Springsted and Lawrence E. Schmidt. University of Notre Dame Press, 2015.

"Whiteness." National Museum of African American History and Culture (NMAACH). Accessed February 28, 2025. https://nmaahc.si.edu/learn/talking-about-race/topics/whiteness.

Williams, Patricia. "Spirit-Murdering the Messenger: The Discourse of Finger-Pointing as the Law's Response to Racism." *University of Miami Law Review* 42, no. 1 (1987). https://repository.law.miami.edu/umlr/vol42/iss1/8.

Yancy, George. *Backlash: What Happens When We Talk About Race Honestly.* With foreword by Cornel West. Rowman & Littlefield, 2018.